CROSS CITY CONNECTIONS

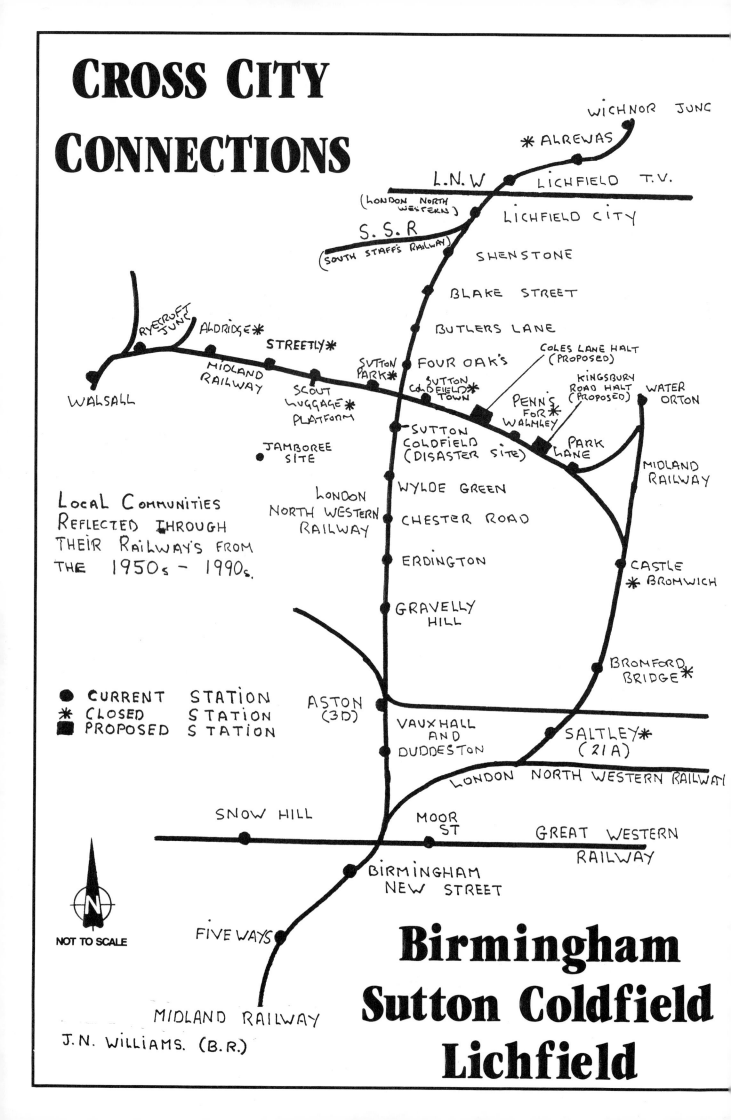

CROSS CITY CONNECTIONS

WICHNOR JUNC

* ALREWAS

L.N.W
(LONDON NORTH WESTERN)

LICHFIELD T.V.

LICHFIELD CITY

S.S.R
(SOUTH STAFFS RAILWAY)

SHENSTONE

BLAKE STREET

BUTLERS LANE

RYECROFT JUNC

ALDRIDGE *

STREETLY *

FOUR OAK'S

COLES LANE HALT
(PROPOSED)

SUTTON PARK *

SUTTON COLDFIELD TOWN *

KINGSBURY ROAD HALT (PROPOSED)

WATER ORTON

MIDLAND RAILWAY

SCOUT LUGGAGE PLATFORM *

PENNS FOR WALMLEY *

PARK LANE

WALSALL

JAMBOREE SITE

SUTTON COLDFIELD (DISASTER SITE)

MIDLAND RAILWAY

Local Communities Reflected Through Their Railways from the 1950s – 1990s.

LONDON NORTH WESTERN RAILWAY

WYLDE GREEN

CHESTER ROAD

ERDINGTON

CASTLE * BROMWICH

GRAVELLY HILL

BROMFORD BRIDGE *

● CURRENT STATION
✳ CLOSED STATION
▪ PROPOSED STATION

ASTON (3D)

VAUXHALL AND DUDDESTON

SALTLEY * (21A)

LONDON NORTH WESTERN RAILWAY

SNOW HILL

MOOR ST

GREAT WESTERN RAILWAY

BIRMINGHAM NEW STREET

N
NOT TO SCALE

FIVE WAYS

Birmingham
Sutton Coldfield
Lichfield

MIDLAND RAILWAY

J.N. WILLIAMS. (B.R.)

CROSS CITY CONNECTIONS

by JOHN BASSETT

BREWIN BOOKS

First published in September 1990 by
K. A. F. Brewin Books, Studley, Warwickshire

Text © John Bassett 1990

ISBN 0 947731 78 4

Typeset in Garamond
by Litho Link Ltd, Welshpool, Powys, Wales

Printed and bound in Great Britain at
The Camelot Press, Trowbridge, Wiltshire.

Contents

Introduction

I am grateful for the help of many, many people, within and outside the railway industry. Those who have been my co-contributors are mentioned by name in the text, whether they have provided verbal, written or photographic material.

In addition to these people, I have appreciated the support of Jack Preston the manuscript reader and adviser, my secretary Brian Redman, and my loving and supportive wife, Joan. Alan Brewin, the Managing Director of Brewin Books, has been very helpful in giving constructive, regular guidance.

Cross City Connections is not meant to be a text-book on Cross City railways within the community in the North Birmingham, Lichfield and Walsall areas, but a lot of research has been done to try and get the things mentioned right. Should you have corrections, points to add, etc. you may care to write to me via the publishers.

John Bassett
Birmingham 1990

Chapter One

WW II influences on the Royal Borough

Cross City Connections is about local communities, including some of their residents who were employed on railways in parts of northern Birmingham, Sutton Coldfield and Staffordshire.

Railways capture and reflect many issues and aspects of local, regional and national life which we may otherwise forget. Our Cross City train link between Lichfield Trent Valley high level station via Sutton Coldfield, Erdington, Birmingham New Street, Kings Norton, Longbridge, Barnt Green then on to Redditch is an example of considerable changes in public and local authority thinking and funding that have taken place to enable the service to happen.

If such a proposal to run a frequent train service between Lichfield Trent Valley and Redditch had been made in, say, 1920, it is very doubtful that it would have been approved by the rival railway companies involved. Putting aside the somewhat sparsely-populated route, the highly competitive and conflicting ideals of the London and North Western Railway and Midland Railway would have prevented such a Cross City link at that time. Passengers travelling from the Staffordshire city of the three spires to the Worcestershire town of Redditch, arriving at Birmingham New Street would need to walk from the LNWR part of the station to the adjacent MR side. Although so close, they were two different worlds. Neither company ran time-tables that took each other's branch lines into consideration.

The issue of two competitive railway companies or two sectors of the same industry combining to provide the communities with a Cross City link comes back into present day public consciousness through the privatisation of the railways. Strange as it may sound, if a financially viable proposition for a Cross City link had been made in 1920 to just one of these companies, the Midland Railway, it may have succeeded. The trains, however, would have gone from Walsall via Aldridge, Streetley, Sutton Park, Sutton Town, Penns for Walmley, Castle Bromwich, Bromford Bridge, Saltley then into the Midland side of New Street and onto Bournville and Redditch.

Early rivalry

A further insight into the competition between the two railway companies was commented upon in the Sutton Coldfield and Erdington News only three months after the Midland line had opened to passenger services on July 1st, 1879. Under the Gossip Column, the writer tells us: "There is a lively system of rivalry going on between the two companies at New Street Station, and it is no uncommon occurrence for passengers to be brought by the line other than that for which they booked, in which case, on the North Western line at any rate, they have to pay over again". The same column, a mere three weeks after the start of the Midland services, gives some reasons why travellers may have selected the alternative older route that opened on June 2nd, 1862 to the LNWR terminus: "There's a fine opening for a steam roller" quips the anonymous journalist, "in front of Sutton Town station on the Midland Railway. Such a wilderness of gravel we have really seldom seen before. If the company leave it to the weather or the slight

traffic they have from the station to crash it into shape, all the traffic will go to the North Western."

Railway photographer Eric Russell comparing local services at Birmingham Snow Hill and New Street, wrote to me saying: "Incidentally, the LNWR, MR and LMS treated New Street in the same way as Snow Hill by the GWR, a terminus for the suburban services to/from the South and the North". Eric goes on "It wasn't till the West Midlands Passenger Transport Executive started the Lichfield/Four Oaks to Longbridge service that a real Cross City service was established". Thinking of Mr. Russell's LNWR, MR, LMS and GWR comparison brings to mind another fascinating alternative proposed by a 'News' reader quoted by Freres in August 1951. The unnamed person stated "If the Great Western had run the Sutton line before the post-Nationalisation paralysis of branch line passenger service development, the facilities would have been more attractive by means of halts at the Girls' High School, Tamworth Lane, and to serve Coles Lane on the other side".

The Sutton Coldfield and Erdington News, apart from pointing fun at the railways — nothing changes — appeared to recognise the importance of the two services to the local population by frequently giving complete train services on both lines. There were 17 on the LNWR up-line to the city and 15 on the down each weekday against the Midlands eight on the up and eight coming back to Sutton Coldfield and Sutton Park and onto Walsall. The Midland also offered a further four trains to Water Orton and three services back from Water Orton. According to the 'News' time-tables the Midland trains did not provide different classes of accommodation whilst the LNWR gave a choice of first, second and third class travel and the daily Government train. The print from John Smith of

Gravelly Hill (Len's of Sutton)

Len's of Sutton (Surrey) shows where the first class accommodation would stop at Gravelly Hill, earlier this century. However, the passengers from the Ladies' first class waiting room on the up platform to Birmingham had to walk past the general waiting room to their first class carriage! The 1914 map of Gravelly Hill station on page 27 of Roger Lea's book "Steaming up to Sutton", 1984, Westwood Press, is worth comparing with John Smith's print.

The Community around the railways

This book reflects changes in our railways and communities in the northern side of Birmingham starting from the 1940s steam era, the diesel years and almost into the 1992 proposed electric Cross City link. As a Suttonian, the subtle childhood influences of railways within the community began with the Midland line that ran near our Jerome Road family home on the Sutton Park route.

School in 1940

Before looking in depth at the northern end of the Cross City link, the Sutton Park line, and some of my experiences as a Railway Chaplain in the West Midlands, I would like to trace some of the childhood impressions that came my way on the council estate that was severed from other Suttonians to the east by the 1879 Midland route. School began at Duke Street primary school, next to Duke Street Hall/Chapel where I later became a member of the Open Brethren group of christians. Day school started with my being put on the rocking horse to stop me crying, but my memory of that event in 1940 was that the crying continued and I was taken off the bucking bronco. For the remainder of my time at the school I never received a further chance to ride on that silent horse, much to my regret. My parents, Albert a cowman and my mother, Polly, did their best for my younger brother, David, who became a BR fireman at Aston Motive Power Depot, and myself, but times were often hard though Dad regularly came home with fresh vegetables. He also grew a variety of crops as his part of digging for victory in the war years. The picture of Dad was taken when he was hoeing the potatoes in the Jerome Road back garden. The left-hand side semi-detached was occupied by Joe Marklew and daughter, Betsy, who was involved with the catering at the Bracebridge Pool Restaurant in Sutton Park.

Albert Bassett in
Jerome Road garden
(John Bassett)

A further regular farm product brought home to supplement his weekly farm labourer wage was milk. It was from milk that he made the family's regular fresh supplies of cheese. This was manufactured by his sitting in an easy chair near the coal fire in the living room and shaking the milk by a long and laborious process until it became a salty cheese.

As a family we benefited from the Sutton Coldfield municipal charities' annual distribution of clothing and footwear; going along to Freeman, Hardy and Willis for example with our voucher. I recall a time when money was short. My mother sacrificed her own shoes so that I had something on my feet to go to school in. Another time, going on a looked-forward-to outing by train from the Park station on the 2.03 pm to Castle Bromwich for the big air show, I ran home from the station because my best clothing on that day was football knicks and a football jumper. I felt so embarassed against my two smart and immaculately turned-out friends with their mother from the private houses in Kathleen Road.

On the corner of Rectory Road and Coleshill Street I sometimes went with my mother to make contributions to the Sutton Coldfield provident dispensary so that the family members could have the services of one of 13 medical officers. In our case, Dr. Peter W. Tait was the family doctor we selected. Amongst the "five peculiar advantages to the poor made available through the scheme was to place medical aid within the means of the working classes!" The scheme also prevented a "sense of degradation which often attends the reception of gratuitous charity". A picture of the dispensary three months after closure was in the 'News' of January 18th, 1957. Back in 1940, 16,936 prescriptions were dispensed, and members paid 1d or 2d a week. Many of the modern arguments for and against private medical care find echoes in the "five peculiar advantages".

The multi-millionaire chauffeur

Although life was not easy it did not seem unhappy to me, as our parents did all they could for us. One highlight of the week in the later 1940s happened on a Sunday afternoon. Sometime after 4.00 pm a number of children, me included, waited outside 27 Jerome Road, the home of Mrs Elizabeth Gilbert. Arthur Barwell from across the road takes up the story: "Mr Alfred Owen, later to become Sir Alfred, called at the home opposite of a widow, Mrs Gilbert, with the weekly rent as an appreciation for the service her husband had given as a gardener to Sir Alfred's father who resided at New Hall. Sir Alfred moved into New Hall some time after his father's death. Some of the Jerome Road children, including John, asked Mr. Owen for a ride in his Bentley car." Mr. Owen came to Mrs. Gilbert's home after helping at the Sutton Coldfield Crusader Class meeting, held in rented property at the rear of Bromwich's, just off the Sutton parade. Our multi-millionaire chauffeur did not seem to be put off by having a group of scoundrels in the back of one of his three valuable Bentleys. There was such a demand for the ride some Sundays he took more than one party for the circular tour down the road, past the two shops, right into Ebrook Road, alongside the former American Airforce Base, past railway carriage cleaner Bill Clayton's home, over the junction with Kathleen Road and Upper Holland Road. On the way along Upper Holland Road, on the left we passed the rear entrance to the Sutton Coldfield Methodist church, then the homes of the Talbots and Carricks, both families associated with the Duke Street Hall. Incidentally, Peter Carrick, Mr. and Mrs. R.C. Carrick's son, designed a very pleasing hall, at the rear of the Sutton Baptist church, where the MacDonald offices now stand in Victoria Road. At the junction with Victoria Road, Coleshill Street and Coleshill Road Mr. Owen turned right past the King's Arms, the garage on the left, then right down Royal Road and the owner-occupied properties with the Midland line at the back, returning to the council houses in Jerome Road. I can still recall Mr. Alfred Owen's friendly face, and his willingness to become an unpaid chauffeur to give the Jerome Road kids a fast, stimulating ride around our short "Silverstone" circuit. Sir Alfred always seemed to be a credit to Jesus Christ, the Saviour he had chosen to follow.

'Any gum, chum?'

As mentioned, in Sir Alfred's tour of the locality we passed the Ebrook Road side entrance; of the American Airforce Base in the town. The yanks, as they were known amongst the locals, moved into buildings which the Birmingham Post of February 23rd, 1938 described as "new schools at Sutton Coldfield to cost more than £50,000". It was part of a "scheme for the reorganisation of elementary schools in the Borough. The Board of Education had approved plans for senior schools in Holland Road which would provide accommodation for 640 children".

Still prior to the AAF moving in, the cost quoted by the Post in June 1940 had risen to £60,000, but the Borough was told as the work had already commenced at that early stage of World War II, "it could carry on until the structure had been roofed in".

Sometime after that the allies moved into the school accommodation and their American uniforms and vehicles became everyday sights in the Royal Borough. Like many other children, I asked the guards at the main gate in Upper Holland Road that faced south parade for "any gum, chum?" Sometimes one was fortunate and received a packet of American chewing gum. Other times the yanks kindly passed on copies of American comics. Although they must have been fed up with our calls for gum, most of the Americans were pleasant. Mrs Joan Price of Jerome Road, who was one of the three Signalwomen working Sutton Park box during some of the war years, remembered the occupation of the school by the Americans. Between 1950–1986 Joan worked as a cleaner in the buildings when it was the Riland Bedford school, leaving before it became Plantsbrook school.

Civic Restaurant

Up south parade from the Air Force Base, before the rear entrance to the Midland Red Garage, and the public baths was the Methodist Church hall which became the town's Civic Restaurant in World War II. My mother worked there for some while as a server. Many times I went for the lunchtime meals and received ample portions from her and other lady servers along the line. Presumably with limited food supplies around, the local authority tried to ensure that the population had access to at least one hot nutritious meal, each weekday. My father, mother, brother and I also benefited on numerous occasions when quantities of surplus main courses and sweets were sent to us, rather than to the pigs.

World War II Queues

Higher up in the town, past Railway Road and Mitfords the jewellers and the Three Tuns on the left, over on the right hand side of the High Street was Miss Bromwich's shop which hundreds of children like me went to once a month. On reflection I do not know where my parents found the 1/6d from, but with it tightly in my hand I waited patiently in the long queue to get into the old-fashioned confectionary shop which had such an inviting mixture of sweet, rich smells. I cannot honestly remember what were my favourites that I exchanged for the family's month of sweet coupons and the 1/6d, but there did seem to be a reasonable collection. However, memories remain of the difficulty of rationing out the month's family supply to last more than the first week let alone the four of five weeks! Mrs. Elsie Turner of Mere Green; told me Miss Bromwich was a member of the bakery family that had a shop in Sutton and Mere Green.

A new treat

Probably the sweetest memory of Sutton parade came not long after the end of World War II. With the demolition of properties in readiness for the development of the Gracechurch Shopping Complex, the Sutton Coldfield News included prints in their issue of July 19th, 1963 of Lipton, Pullars of Perth, Maypole and my favourite choice — Trow's Milk Bar. I believe it was a Sunday afternoon. Children in the town knew the yanks often had this, to us a rare treat but could only dream about it. At least up to then. Again, in a queue we gradually went in the shop to a new experience. Having taken my money I was given a spoon, with one scoop of vanilla ice cream in a glass dish. How lovely it tasted! It was a completely fresh taste, enjoyed in the enclosed milk bar tabled area of Trow's at the rear of the building, with views over the back gardens to the LNWR line into Sutton Coldfield station.

Holly trail

An annual pilgrimage for me and some other Jerome Road youngsters was the visit to the council depot at Blackroot Pool for the family's complimentary bundle of Christmas holly. It was always difficult to get the important festive item home because of the holly branches being long and prickly. The normal method of transporting the holly was to drag it the two miles home across the grass near the paddling area, over the meadow platt, through the main gates, down Park Road, under the LNWR railway bridge, past Hastilows Removals and Tudor Rose Coaches, where we often rested to view the latest addition to the company's stock. We must have looked a right sight crossing the parade and down Victoria Road. The surprise was that there were still berries for my mother's requirements of Christmas decorations on reaching the Jerome Road home!

Lineside Awakenings

Having painted a word picture of some background memories that I associate with Sutton Coldfield in the 1940s, I go back to those early railway influences on me in Jerome Road. A disturbing World War II factor for many residents in our road, Ebrook Road, Coles Lane, Kathleen Road, Royal Road and Coleshill Road was that of being woken during the night by a wheezing, crawling, stalling, then stopping steam locomotive on the 1/100 gradient. Once the clanging and clattering of the umpteen wagons and trucks had stopped from the long and heavy goods train, there was usually a lull until the locomotive had regained sufficient pressure then, with a sharp whistle, much wheel slipping and skyward sparks from the freight engine's chimney, the tired footplate crew encouraged the reluctant beast towards the 1925 closed Sutton Town station and onto Sutton Park station. Commenting on that type of situation, Sutton Park Station Master, Mr. E.J. Hankin said: "Trains failing to get up the incline had to be either pushed up from the rear by power from Water Orton, or pulled from the front by an engine from Sutton Park under the wrong line order". An alternative to those procedures given by Mr. Hankin was mentioned to me by Joan Price, the signalwoman at Sutton Park between 1942-46, who lived in our road. She recalled, "the train guard would put detonators on the down side track" (to Sutton Park and Walsall) "¾ mile behind the halted goods train to protect it. Then the train engine having

PW staff going down the Sutton Park incline (*R. Paddison*)

taken half to Sutton Park returned for the remainder of the train. Once the signalperson was satisfied the train was complete he/she would arrange for it to continue its journey".

Fireman, later guard, George Stokes told me that the engines "slipped to a stand because of leaves on the line and wet damp rails". Joe Evitts, a Saltley driver, often fired locos on the line towards the end of the steam. His regular driver for two and a half years was the late Sid Watkins. Joe remembers them working a freight towards Sutton Park, "when our class 8F had a "blow up" (became short of steam) and stuck on the incline because of rain and leaves on the rails. The guard came up and halved the train, then we took half, leaving it in Sutton Park yard. We later went back to collect the rest". Permanent Way engineer Robert Paddison's print shows the severity of the incline between Sutton Park station and Coles Lane, as pw staff walk towards the Sutton Town station buildings.

Another awakening families like ours in Jerome Road, and other parts of Northern Birmingham and Sutton Coldfield, had during the second world war was from the frequent sound of air raid sirens. Sometimes the darkened night sky was lit up with evidence of German bombing in Birmingham. Strangely enough to a child's mind it was part of life finding oneself waking up in a small warm galvanised world of the garden-sited air-raid shelter, on bedding hurriedly taken the 20 yards from home. With the all-clear, spiders and a variety of creepy-crawlies were shaken off the bedding as the Jerome Road and Ebrook Road council house tenants left their second homes. There was frequently an eeriness in the air as the families fumbled their way back to the bricks and mortar house.

Thinking again of the trains held up on the Midland line gradient, Elsie Turner, who at the time lived the other side of the rails where Coleshill Road and Reddicap Hill met, wrote of the danger such trains could bring for Suttonians. "In the late 30s and 40s the line became increasingly used for freight trains, and on the very long ones you would find two engines used on the long incline from Penns, up to Sutton, especially at night, when the line was at its busiest, when there was only one engine, it would stop for about ten minutes opposite our cottages and build up steam. Because of this, during the war we looked anxiously because, as they fired up, there would be a red glow and, during the nightly raids, this was a great worry to us. A stick of bombs was dropped in the fields of New Hall, also there was a Battery in Walmley Ash Road".

Mobile guns

One of the reasons it has taken me seven years to complete this book has been the need to collate many vital eye witness reports of five decades or more of individual experiences in north Birmingham, Warwickshire and Staffordshire. Inevitably, accounts are included that cannot be checked at the time, but readers subsequently shed more light onto a subject, occasionally supported by photographs. Mrs. Turner goes on to mention a fascinating rumour that was circulating in the war years, but no photographic evidence has come my way yet! "Locals believe there was a Bofars AA gun travelling up and down the line at night. How true this was I don't know, but I do know our shelters were peppered with shrapnel". Elsie told me of the use she made of the trains on that route. "We had relations who lived at Alum Rock, and I remember well how we used to catch the train at the old Town station and go to Saltley, then walk up the Rock to our destination. When the Town station closed in 1925, we used the Midland Wharf (Sutton Park) but it was a longer walk from the bottom of Reddicap Hill. As the bus service came to Sutton and became more frequent, so the passenger service to the Midland line declined".

Shortly after the end of World War II residents either side of the incline, as well as the animals at New Hall Farm run by Mr. Cashmore, had another awakening. There was a particularly severe winter with extremely deep snowdrifts. To

help keep the southwest/midland/north freight corridor open via Sutton Park, a powerful turbine-type snow-clearing vehicle on rails came up the gradient causing excessive noise and consternation in the railside neighbourhood. However, it achieved its objective of clearing the line. This same instance appears to be recorded in Kingsbury Rail 150 1839-1989 by the Kingsbury Station Committee, on page 10. "The bad weather of 1947 had turned into an equally bad early spring. It was the first week in March and snow was still falling. Snowdrifts and the problems they caused were being investigated at the time by doing trials with a jet engine mounted on a wagon. Not only did it clear the snow but it also blew away the ballast".

Tamworth — double vision

Growing up and watching the varied selection of former Midland Railway, London North Western, London Midland and Scottish, and later standard British Railway steam locos through the gap facing our house between the houses that backed onto that line, encouraged my interest in railways, and steam locos in particular. Two of my favourite train-spotting locations were at Tamworth and Nechells. Tamworth was reached on the Midland "Red" 110 or X99 services. Standing in the station fields by the River Anker, I waited with many other spotters to see what high-speed locomotives came after the "clanger" shout had gone up from the waiting enthusiasts. The name "Gricer" was to be added to the dictionary in a future decade. Engines on the west coast main line could include Stanier Class 5s, Patriot, Jubilee, Claughton and Royal Scots. The Anglo-Scottish services were usually powered by "Princess Royal" 4-6-2 7P machines or one of the 38 "Princess Coronation" class including the "City-of-Birmingham" 46235, shedded at Crewe North, and the "City of Lichfield" 46250,

The late Mr. E.R. Morten's picture catches a Garratt on a Birmingham via Tamworth to Toton through goods in LMS days (*E.R. Morten*)

based at the time at Carlisle Upperby. Many a time, in company with friends, I went into the Tamworth station cafe for a thirst-quenching bottle of pop. Terry and Meryl Smith provide a similar facility on Tamworth low level station these days, but the number of enthusiasts are far less. A well-known name amongst parliamentarians was instrumental in getting Tamworth on the LNW Railway map. In Tamworth Corporation's 1958 book "Borough by prescription" by Henry Wood (p. 112) it states that "The Trent Valley line was opened in 1847". The first turf was cut by Sir Robert Peel, when Prime Minister, in a field of his own adjoining the Staffordshire Moor, at a ceremony attended by George Stephenson on November 13th, 1845.

Not only did the spotters benefit from Sir Robert's vision on the low level line, they often suffered double vision when trains appeared simultaneously on the LNWR route and on the former Midland Main line on the high level between the South West, Midlands, North and North East. Page 4 of "Kingsbury Rail 150" declares that the first locomotives on the Birmingham and Derby Junction Railway (the high level line) included 12 2-2-2 engines with 5'6" diameter driving wheels. The named engines included "Barton" and "Tamworth". The top level expresses not long after nationalisation in 1948 tended to be pulled by Jubilee and Class "5" engines. Interest for the enthusiasts was at least as great towards the considerable number of freight power was noted including the ubiquitous Class 5s, Class 8s and the 155 ton, 10 cwt 2-6-6-2 T Beyer-Garratt machines, introduced by the LMS in 1927/30 to pull their long, heavy coal trains. They were shedded about that time at Toton or Hasland. Over 40 years later during my visits to Tamworth signal box, the Chargeman's office, the refreshment kiosk, the booking office, S & T fault-finding team or the PW cabin, as the Railway Chaplain in the West Midlands employed by the Railway Mission, some of the heavy freight trains that come briskly over the high level bring back memories of the Beyer-Garratt engines with their long trains of coal trucks and a guard's van that seemed to be half a mile behind. The one main difference, even allowing for poisonous diesel fumes these days, was the blanket of black smoke that enclosed part of the following train and station buildings, bringing on coughing fits for the less adjusted lungs at the scene. Incidentally, the Sectional Appendix gave the distance in October, 1960 as 1080 yards between Tamworth LL and HL signal boxes with a 15 mph restriction.

Through the palings

The other favourite spotting location I went to was usually combined with a visit to my Uncle Bill Walker's at Washwood Heath who was a railway Ganger at Adderley Park. Alighting by train or bus in Aston, I walked up Holborn Hill to near the junction with Long Acre. On the right hand side of the hill was a line of wooden palings, or they may have been railway sleepers, which had conveniently-placed holes for inquisitive train spotters. Beyond the wooden boundary lay the dark, damp and smokey Aston Motive Power Depot. There always seemed to be a pall of smoke and steam around, stopping number takers from getting the loco's vital statistics. Some spotters climbed on to the top of the fence to get a better view. The houses in Holborn Hill behind the enthusiasts were terraced. As mentioned before, my brother David worked at Aston MPD, 3D. He told me, "when a light engine came onto the shed, the train crew took it to the coaling plant, where the fireman got off 'phoning the shed office. The driver took the engine on a bit further to the coaling stage. The fireman advised the office person of the loco number and job number just completed. The office sent a disposal team of a driver and fireman who were on shed duties. The disposal staff coaled, watered and cleaned the fire of the engine before taking it on to its allocated shed road for the next turn of duty. There was a steam raiser employed on each shift to make sure each engine had sufficient water and coal while it was on Aston shed".

Another train crew team David advised me about checked the engine's oil levels, sand, lights, and put the necessary tools on. From memory the "tool kit comprised one bucket, a full can of detonators, spanners, one shovel, a pick and two lamps". For a while after David was recovering from a road accident, his duties included working as an assistant in the Aston hostel, located off Long Acre Road. Train crews from other depots, including Scottish footplatemen, were provided with small individual, though sparse, bedrooms, basic washing facilities and twenty four hours canteen service. The hostel assistant woke up visiting train crews at the requested time in readiness for the next duty. When David was away from his depot he went to a number of hostels, including Edge Hill

Something of the atmosphere around the 3D coaling plant is caught by Ted "Button" Higgs' shot of 70047, with driver Harry Hennesey and fireman Tony Shelley *(Ted Higgs)*

where the foreign crews had to cook their own breakfast, and their bedrooms were small with oldish beds and one chair each. The hostel buildings themselves were in the main very old. John Hooper in his book "London Midland Scottish Railway, locomotive allocations, the last day 1947" Irwell Press, 1989, gives details of the 7932 engines of the LMS, the day before nationalisation. At the time, the number of locos at the following sheds with their codes were:

Aston (3D) 49; Bescot (3A) 74; Monument Lane (3E) 32; Walsall (3C) 60; Bournville (21B) 34; Burton (17B) 111; Saltley (21A) 181; and Westhouses (18B) 52.

Nechells views

Walking on up Holborn Hill and partly along Aston Church Road I came to my second favourite location, through a small gate on the left. I liked that place because few other spotters went there. It has the Midland main line and Sutton Park services, trains on the Aston-Stetchford route and, occasionally, pre-public views of new or refurbished stock from the carriage and wagon works, including stock for overseas railways. The environment in Nechells was far less attractive than the Anker Valley but it had its own attractiveness to a schoolboy spotter. The uphill and downdale route to Uncle Bill's continued up to Washwood Heath and his Ash Terrace railway terraced house, with outside communal toilets and washing facilities.

Seeking employment

Not long before I was due to leave the Sutton Coldfield Technical College in Lichfield Road, Sutton Coldfield in April 1950, and start work, my parents arranged with my Uncle Bill a visit to the Adderley Park signal box to meet the duty signalman to talk about my interest in railways and whether there could be an appropriate opening for me on the railway.

I still recall a London bound express roaring past the box, leaving a cloud of smoke in the cutting with a smell of sulphur drifting back into the box. It was a bit of an unreal visit with a chance to tap out the bell codes and pull over the heavy signal levers, under the observing signalman and my smiling uncle.

Four Oaks Station Master John Shallis (*John Bassett*)

Shortly afterwards I took my vacancy card for a Junior Porter position with me up to Four Oaks Station, on the 1884 section of the former LNWR branch between New Street and Lichfield City via Sutton Coldfield.

I was met by Bristolian Station Master John Shallis. He showed me round the attractive country station with its two main platforms, buildings, two bays, gardens, signalbox, goods weighbridge and goods yard. He explained it was an important commuter station with a number of Birmingham New Street trains starting and terminating there. With pride he showed me the Best Kept Station Shield won by Four Oaks in 1949 against other stations of the Birmingham Division of the LMR. In addition to busy commuter periods each weekday morning and evening there were daily stopping tripper goods trains and a considerable assortment of weekday parcels for delivery and despatch. The local railway station in 1950 was an important integrated part of the community, with the majority of folk depending on public transport to get them and their belongings around.

The importance and respect shown to local shopkeepers at the time was indicated by my parents' guidance to use Mrs. Sarah Crockett, who owned the grocer, confectioner and tobacconist business in one of the two shops at the bottom of Jerome Road, as one of my two referees for the job.

40364 speeding towards Four Oaks (*J. Hicks*)

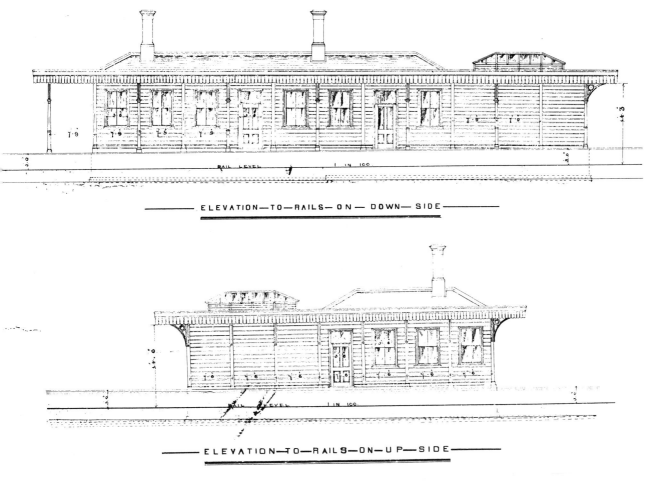

— ELEVATION—TO—RAILS—ON—DOWN—SIDE —

— ELEVATION—TO—RAILS—ON—UP—SIDE —

Four Oaks buildings (see photographs on pages 12 & 13)

As I contemplated a railway career in 1950, a cheap day ticket from Four Oaks to Birmingham was 1s 2d, from Sutton to the city 1s 1d, with a similar fare from Sutton Park and Penns to New Street. It cost 1s 6d from Penns to Walsall, 1s 2d from the Park to Walsall, and 1s 6d for those travelling from Sutton to Lichfield City. F.J. Hall Ltd. in Four Oaks Goods Yard Station Drive sold coal, coke, anthracite, firelighters, logs, lime, fertilizers, hop manure etc. The estimated Sutton Coldfield population of 47,440 at the time could see "12 o'clock High" with Gregory Peck at the Odeon, "Boys in Brown" (A), starring Jack Warner and Richard Attenborough at the Empress, Sutton, while "Neptune's Daughter" (U) featuring Esther Williams was being screened at the Pavilion, Wylde Green. The revived interest in football that followed the cessation of World War II continued unabated with admission to adults of 1/-d to watch Boldmere St. Michael's play Kidderminster Harriers in the Birmingham and District League. New ration books in 1950 could be obtained from the Ministry of Food by going to the YMCA Assembly Room, High Street, Sutton, the temporary public library in Mere Green Road, or at the Ambulance Department in Boldmere Road. With the opening of the Sutton Coldfield television station on December 15th, 1949, a growing number of people rented or bought television sets. In the late 1940s there was a demonstration of working TV sets in the Assembly Hall, King Edward Square of King Edwards Square, depending on which side of the road you stand! I went to the demonstration, going from one black and white set to the next to see the same programme. Just at the top of the square, the Town Council in 1950 was putting pressure on the appropriate authorities to

change the postal address from Sutton Coldfield, Birmingham to Sutton Coldfield, Warwickshire.

Presumably Mr. Shallis was not too put off because a week or two later "Enoch", the name he gave me, received a request to go for a railway medical with the "Company Doctor" at Derby. Back in 1950 there were a few through services from New Street to Burton-on-Trent via Sutton Coldfield with at least one going all the way to Derby.

The fine pan shot of 40364 was taken between Sutton Coldfield and Four Oaks. My father as a cowman for Farmer Mr. Cattell, told me that when he worked in the fields near the section of railway, the push and pull trains presumably before or during WWII, were invariably on time. "You could set your watch by them", he advised me. Feeling important with my free rail pass I caught the 9.17 a.m. from Sutton Coldfield which took 5 minutes for the 1¼ mile uphill run through the tunnel, under the Sutton Park line, behind Moat House, the Sutton Coldfield Technical College, Bishop Vessey's Grammar School, over Tamworth Road, Little Sutton Lane, then up to Four Oaks Station, where I looked out on to a very tidy, clean station. The short non-corridor train reached Lichfield City at 9.39 but had a 27 minute connection wait at Trent Valley high level station. With stops at Alrewas and Barton and Walton we arrived at Burton-on-Trent for 10.32 before reaching the former Midland Railway centre at Derby by 10.53, taking 1 hour 36 minutes for 31½ miles. Derby was a second heaven for the steam enthusiast with much rail activity to see in and around the station, works and loco sheds. The white coated doctor examined me, asking questions about my health. Apparently being fit enough I started at Four Oaks Station not long afterwards.

Chapter Two

Early BR days at Four Oaks

The full staff establishment at Four Oaks in April 1950 was: Station Master Shallis, who had two shift Foremen being Bob Evans with Junior Porter Ron Gardiner and Alfie Webb for whom I worked. There were two Signalmen, J. Butler and J. Gilbert in a box that was open at one time from 5.00 a.m.–11.45 p.m., separated on early and later shifts on weekdays by middle turn Porter/Signalman Phil Boston. Dennis Cartmale was another Four Oaks Signalman for a while. A relief Signalman was Albert Gregory of Sutton Coldfield who later went to live in Australia.

Tom Compton a fanatical Aston Villa supporter was the Goods Clerk based in the weighbridge who travelled from his Great Barr home. The Booking Clerks mainly seemed to come from the Lichfield area like Del Pritchard, Jeff Webb and Richard Coleman. Del now works at Bescot, Richard is in the LMR HQ at Stanier House in Birmingham. Richard is a regular member of the Railway Mission meetings held in Stanier House. Jeff retired from Stanier House in 1989. Another former Four Oaks Junior Clerk who has visited my New Street Station office is Ken Chadwick now employed by Thomas Cook.

Late breakfast time heralded the weekday arrival of three rail parcel lorries based at Sutton Coldfield to deliver parcels in and around Four Oaks. Another two who started their weekday tasks at Four Oaks were the Carriage Cleaners, both called Bill. After their Four Oaks work and breakfast they travelled down to the Vauxhall and Duddeston Carriage Works to complete their working day. The works was demolished after being partly blown down in 1989. Four Oaks was the booking on point for some Passenger Guards. Mr. Shallis told me they were, "Albert Breakwell, Freddy Harris, Billy Hart and Jimmy Robbins". Some of them such as Billy Hart carried out relief Foreman duties when Alf or Bob were on holiday or off ill. Billy Hart recalled that guard Joe Felton also booked on at our station. Although not under the supervision of Mr. Shallis the station had a permanent way gang working to Ganger Jack Gilbert. Mr. Shallis remembers the, "gang including J. Hatton, C. Read and W. Roberts".

THE LOCAL RAILWAY STATION:
centre for employment

So Four Oaks station in 1950 provided full or part time railway employment for about 25 persons each weekday, plus those who worked in the coal merchants/builders offices at the station. That kind of employment pattern could be repeated nationwide reflecting the importance of the local railway station in the community shortly after the Second World War. Some vestiges of WWII were still around when I started that April, 1950, at Four Oaks as a junior porter. Every so often all the staff received packages of foodstuffs such as margarine and sugar because we belonged and provided an essential service to the community. I recall being very proud on arriving home with my parcel of goodies for my mother, paid out of my weekly pay packet.

THE EARLY MORNING WALK TO WORK

I used to leave home about 5.15 a.m. on the early turn ready to book on for the 6.00 a.m. start. The 1¾ miles journey was partly along the then A.38, now A.5127. One morning having passed Tamworth Road, it was dark and wet. As I walked along trying to stop the rain getting down my neck I became aware of a figure slowly approaching me near the curb. There on a slow moving cycle was a headless man! I did not know what to do as the body and cycle came up to me. Fortunately in the light of a distant street lamp I just caught sight of a man's face peering out of the top of his mac, also seeking to avoid the rain. Sometimes when I felt the need for company I went round to the first house in Ebrook Road, Sutton Coldfield, for 4.30 a.m. and walked to Four Oaks station with Duddeston based cleaner Billy Clayton. He told me some fascinating stories of finding objects including money, whilst cleaning carriages. His colleague, another Bill, lived nearby in Coles Lane. I think the other Bill sometimes waited at the closed Sutton station for a lift from a crew on a light engine going up to Four Oaks or Lichfield City.

Four Oaks Goods Clerk, Tom Compton *(John Bassett)*

The first task of the two Bills and the Junior Porter on early turn focused on preparation and departure of the 6.10 a.m. Four Oaks–New Street service calling at Sutton Coldfield, Wylde Green, Chester Road, Erdington, Gravelly Hill, Aston, Vauxhall and Duddeston, where the tickets were collected and checked, then New Street. Whereas the two Bills could be seen in the upside bay sweeping out the 6-10 non-corridor stock with brush and pan, I was in the upside platform booking office lighting the stove fire and selling workmen daily or weekly returns mainly to Aston and New Street, for that first service from Four Oaks. The Junior Porters on the early shift soon knew the regular 6.10, 6.45 and 7.17 a.m. passengers and which persons required a weekly cycle ticket! The cycle shed was removed in 1989, but it was well used in the 1950s. The Booking Clerk arrived to take over the booking office duties at about 7.20 a.m. In between the Birmingham departures the Junior continued lighting coal fires in the Foreman's hut, Station Master's office, on the downside, and the waiting rooms. The first service, early in the 50's from New Street arrived at Four Oaks by 6.59 a.m. Another glimpse of the importance of rail transport at that time to local shops, was the arrival on that train of boxes of fish from Grimsby for Turrell's the Mere Green fishmongers and fresh cream products for bakeries and cafes.

SUTTON LINE EXPRESS

With the morning service of the 7.45, 7.58, 8.18 and 8.28 a.m. we saw the business and executive travellers replacing the overall and lunchbag passengers of the first three Birmingham bound trains. The 8.18 a.m. was the only train that omitted any stops on its way to New Street, being known as the "Express". However the use of a few express services on the earlier portion of line between Birmingham and Sutton Coldfield is shown in a February, 1870, timetable in "Steaming up to Sutton". In the 1952 timetable for instance, the 8.18 a.m. took 28 minutes from Four Oaks, not stopping at Chester Road, Erdington, Gravelly Hill and Aston. My regular Foreman, Alf Webb, who booked on at 5.45 a.m., was mainly occupied with shunting duties involving the 6.10, 7.45 and 8.28 Four Oaks starters. However, as the light engine for the 6.10 usually driven by Monument Lane men like Bill Corns or Harold Onions arrived by 5.30 a.m. they had frequently got the coaching stock into the bay before the Foreman arrived and the train warmed up for passengers such as Len Goldingay who travelled to Aston.

British Rail has its own internal postal service with some letters travelling in unsealed envelopes, which could be reused many times. From my observations on the early and late turns, the foreman frequently knew of management decisions before the station master! If asked why he was in the S.M.'s office he was of course checking all was well for the station master shortly to come on duty.

In between shunting, letter opening and seeing off trains, the Foreman began writing down details of parcels not yet on the lorry driver's list. After 7 a.m. Tom Compton, the Goods Clerk could be seen around the yard. When the SM was short of platform staff, Tom would give a hand with closing carriage doors and getting trains away on time. Ganger Gilbert also helped in that way on occasions, mainly in the evenings or on Saturdays. About the same time as Tom was around, Phil Boston, the red faced and jovial Porter Signalman, could be seen riding down the island platform on his large upright cycle to begin his porter duties until mid day when he took over the signal box work for the afternoon.

RAILBORNE PARCEL TRAFFIC

From about 8.30 in the morning the focus of attention at Four Oaks moved to the downside office where the Station Master and Booking Clerk could be found. The Lorry Drivers from Sutton Coldfield, including Alf Archer, Harry Bennett and Les Shelley were helped to load up parcels for Four Oaks,

Four Oaks Ganger Jack Gilbert by the footbridge *(William Gilbert)*

Mere Green, Blake Street, Streetly, Little Aston and Canwell. In the early 1950's British Railways held a considerable slice of the parcel traffic conveyed in England, because the majority of places, large and small, had a station. Four Oaks was a busy parcel distribution and despatch centre. The considerable volume and variety of parcels and products seen on the 3 vehicles each weekday from the station showed the vast contrast to the scene 40 years later, with no sign of the 1884 downside buildings, let alone the parcels traffic. One recalls calling out the address of the parcel's recipients to the Foreman or clerk who wrote it down on the driver's delivery sheet. Some of the mail order traffic came from Baldock and Belper. During my duties in the late 1980's and early 90's as a Chaplain I see the station staff putting parcel details onto the computer

Working Timetable – Freight Trains 1957

Aston Jct - Lichfield City Freight Timetable

		4.45 a.m. empties Aston goods - Wichnor	Light engine	9.10 a.m. Curzon St.	10.40 a.m. empties Aston goods to Blackwell	10.40 a.m. empties Aston goods to Blackwell
Weekdays		a.m.	a.m.	a.m. SX	a.m. SX	a.m. SO
Down Line Train No.			166	162		
Aston Junction	dep	4.50	6.9	9.17	10.46	10.46
Erdington	arr			9.30	10.57	10.57
	dep			10.53	11.55	11.55
Sutton Coldfield	arr			11.05		
	dep	5.10		12.02	12.10	12.10
Four Oaks	arr					
	dep		6.22			
Blake Street	arr			12.24		
	dep					
Lichfield	arr		6.35			
	dep	5.45			12.50	12.45

		10.20 p.m. Wichnor to Aston Goods 161 MX	9.45 a.m. Wichnor to Aston Goods	166 SX	166 SO	162 SX	9.45 a.m. Tibshelf to Aston Goods	10.00 p.m. Wichnor to Aston Goods Sundays 161
Weekdays Train No.		a.m.					p.m.	a.m.
Upline Lichfield City	dep	12.6	9.40	10.40	10.40		3.40	12.01
Shenstone	arr.			10.55	10.55			
	dep.			11.05	11.50	2.50		
Blake St.	arr					3.00		
	dep					3.15		
Four Oaks	arr		10.09*	11.25	12.10	3.20		
	dep		10.24*	12.24	12.55	3.35		
Sutton Coldfield	arr			12.30	1.01	3.41		
	dep	12.43	10.29	1.30	2.00	4.28	4.15	12.38
Chest Rd	arr							
	dep							
Erdington	arr			1.45	2.15	4.41		
	dep			3.35	4.05	4.51		
Aston Junction	arr						4.30	
	dep	12.58	10.48	3.46	4.16	5.01		12.53

* stops or shunts for other trains to pass

(Freight time table)

controlled machine which states the cost and the train service for the Red Star/Night Star item. It also prints the label/s. Not in the 1950's — it was all individual effort, with the need for clear writing.

THE GOODS SIDE

Another feature of rail centred life in the 1950's all over the country was the freight business and the daily tripper goods trains. Each weekday morning T166 between Lichfield City and Curzon Street arrived with full loads of coal for F.J. Hall, Weavers, which was later taken over by Evesons. Hall and Co. had a private siding on the upside by the 629 yard carriage siding. Other loads that Goods Clerk Tom Compton had to deal with included stock-feed potatoes, sugarbeet pulp, trucks of bricks for Joburns and bags of cement for a local builder. The loco was usually a class 3 or 4 freight engine, but on occasions a class 5 Stanier. Brother David recalled going light engine to Lichfield City, where they shunted the yard. After breakfast they shunted at Shenstone and Four Oaks.

Retired drivers Ken Beasley and Bill Dobson had strong memories of 162 and 166. They recalled that "Erdington had 21 coal roads and was the most important coal yard on the branch". We shall reconsider trippers 162 and 166 when we think about Sutton Coldfield station later in the book, but for now we return to the Four Oaks goods yard. Acting Foreman Billy Hart used "to mark the empty trucks and wagons with "MT" so that he could pick them out ready for marshalling, rather than peering down at the small labels on each wagon". Various station staff assisted the Goods Clerk to fold the large tarpaulin sheets from open trucks to be returned to Curzon Street depot by goods train. George Stephens, a Junior Porter after me in 1954-57 at Four Oaks remembered, "occasionally helping Tom unload the station coal from a truck left in the downside bay near the goods shed". Arthur Attenborough reminded me that Foreman Bob Evans, who lived at Mere Green, was widely known on the Railway "for his watch and clock repairs". "Mr. Evans rode to work on a Bantam, then later a Sun m/c", commented George.

The Signal box and goods yard from the upside sidings *(William Gilbert)*

FOUR OAKS STATION ENVIRONMENT

Folk who never knew the buildings at and around the station would find it hard to imagine the scene as they now look at the large free car parks with Four Oaks House beyond.

In the early 1950's, four terraced railway cottages, now the site of the car park facing the downside waiting shelter, were occupied by Mr. and Mrs. Shallis and daughter Patricia, P.W. Ganger Jack Gilbert with his wife Lily and daughter Peggy, Traffic Inspector Griffin and his wife. The last cottage, nearest the station in the photo, was the home of railway widow, Mrs. Holmes, and Alf and Doris Remblance. The station master had a double fronted tenancy with two front rooms, kitchen and three bedrooms, whilst the three remaining cottages had single frontages with one living room, kitchen and three bedrooms. Each cottage had an outside toilet.

Stanier 2-6-4T No. 42441 on the 4.07 p.m. train to Birmingham, standing opposite the timber goods shed with prize winning gardens to the right *(Eric S. Russell)*

LMR view of the Four Oaks 1884 buildings *(B.R. (M))*

TIMETABLE COMPARISONS   Time Table comparisons

August 1945

Upside to Birmingham

	Am	Pm SO	*		
Four Oaks dep.	11.22	12.28	1.12	2.17	4.37
B'ham. N. St. Arr.	11.56	1.6	1.45	2.50	5.10

* Four Oaks starter

August 1952

	Am	Pm SO	*		
	11.22	12.32	1.12	2.00	4.29
	11.56	1.06	1.46	2.33	5.11

Downside to Four Oaks/Lichfield

August 1945

	Am	Pm *	SE	SO			SO	SE
B'ham. N. St. Dep.	8.50	12.10	12.25	12.42	1.6	2.15	4.18	4.45
Four Oaks Arr.	9.24	12.41	12.59	1.13	1.37	2.52	4.49	5.16

August 1952

	Am	Pm *	SE	SO	SO	SE	SO	SO	SE
B'ham. N. St. Dep.	8.50	12.10	12.25	12.45	1.15	2.35	2.45	4.18	4.48
Four Oaks Arr.	9.22	12.41	12.57	1.16	1.46	3.5	3.15	4.49	5.22

* Four Oaks terminating

In the reasonable size downside goods complex where the other car park is now situated, was the goods weighbridge across from a number of small wooden buildings housing the coal merchant's admin staff in the goods yard. The first wooden building on the left in the goods yard was used by Evesons. Mr. Shallis told me, "Miss Bishop was in charge, and Tommy Gardiner next door was the manager of F.J. Hall. Betty Lewis and Jean Johnson were his admin staff. Jim Stacey drove for F.J. Hall and Charlie Thorpe for Evesons". George Stephens remembered, "Graham Warrington was a strong F.J. Hall coalman". In later years Mr. Shallis, "used one of the coal bunkers next to F.J. Hall to keep my car". On the down platform beyond the main station buildings and the metal trelliswork footbridge was the Foreman's hut with a coal burning stove and cooking ring. In the next longer wooden building towards the signal box were the Guards' and Porters' lockers. I kept dusters and firelighters, amongst other things, in my locker. The last buildings at the end of the down platform was an even larger timber goods shed.

"The building," George said, "was the goods shed used as a store place. We chopped wood in it. The railways kept sacks in there which they hired to farmers to put grain in". I recall that disinfectant from the goods shed was used to clean out elephant boxes at Four Oaks which has transported the animals to Sutton Coldfield for circus performances in Sutton Park.

A RURAL STATION ATMOSPHERE

Once the lorries had departed with their parcel traffic and late breakfasts finished, Four Oaks Station in the early 1950's became a quiet rural place with long gaps between services similar to that offered at the end of WWII.

STATION CLEANING DUTIES

The two Junior Porters, one on either shift, had responsibility for the cleaning of the up or down side station buildings. In 1950/51 I looked after the main 1884 building that was on the downside.

The April 21st, 1884 plan as shown was made five months before the Sutton Coldfield to Lichfield City extension opened to Goods in September, and passenger traffic began just prior to Christmas on the December 15th, 1884. The downside shows the accommodation I cleaned being, left to right:

Parcels office which included a weighing machine, table, cupboard, shelves around the walls, storage area, labels etc., and the first window.

Station Master's Office: The next two windows were in the Station Master's office which had a sloping desk, book case, book shelves, with pigeon holes above. The telephone on the desktop gave the public access to passenger and goods information. The SM, Foreman, Booking Clerks and Junior Porters were all expected to be able to read timetables and give fares to local and distant locations. I often used to spend part of my lunchbreaks looking up routes and timetables, trying to memorise the principal services. There was an old comfortable wooden chair, open fireplace and counter with date printing machine.

Booking, Waiting and Toilet Facilities: Near the machine was a hatch which enabled the passengers in the combined booking hall and waiting room to book their tickets to stations up to Lichfield TV, Burton on Trent, Derby and further away. The waiting room had a number of hanging pictures showing destinations accessible by train. The floor covering and that in the adjacent ladies waiting room was brown lino with long strong wooden benches to match. The ladies' accommodation included a toilet suite. The remainder of the downside building was the men's toilets. The brass pipework in the men's toilet paid to be polished but looked terrible when left for a day or two.

Upside buildings: The external view of the upside building per the April, 1884 drawing is still easily recognisable, although the gent's toilet block that took up half the accommodation has been considerably altered. The former lean-to shelter over the ticket hatch was commented upon by Mr. R.W. Powell Hendry in correspondence with me about the architecture of the downside building at Four Oaks Station. He wrote, "In a normal building of this size, there would have been a booking office for the staff and a separate booking hall/waiting room for passengers. I cannot produce an explanation as to why this station is odd, but it suggests that there is some curious background. It may be that all tickets were issued from the buildings on the other platform, a ticket hatch was cut in the end, and a lean-to added". Mr. Hendrey and his father, Dr. R. Preston Hendrey, the joint authors of "An historical survey of selected LMS stations with layouts and illustrations — Volume One", kindly agreed to copies of relevant material in their book being used. OPC, the publishers, also agreed.

Downside building from the driveway, March, 1949 (*Eric S. Russell*)

Upside building in March, 1949 *(Eric S. Russell)*

In 1989 major alterations were completed at Four Oaks including the provision of a longer ticket office within the 1884 upside building. The covered accommodation leading to the booking office window includes a waiting area with a window facing the footbridge, in place of the lean-to, as seen in Rob Selvey's print on p. 00.

JUNIOR PORTERS

The Junior Porters overlapped at lunchtime for a couple of hours. My opposite number, Ron, soon moved onto a locomotive fireman position, eventually becoming a driver at Saltley. Other Junior Porters at Four Oaks included Fred and Billy Bell from Ebrook Road, Sutton Coldfield. Mr. Shallis related the story of, "Billy cleaning the floor of the ladies waiting room one day. He had his face towards the floor and courteously said 'Good morning, Madam' as the person walked from the ladies toilets. Bill was later embarrassed to find that 'Madam' was Porter/Signalman Phil Boston". As already mentioned, George Stephens was a Junior Porter at the station. George was the Midland TUCC Superstaff award winner in 1989, working at Butlers Lane before moving to New Street station on revenue collecting duties.

LOCO RUNNING-IN DUTIES

An interesting locomotive feature about the 12.10 ex New Street and return 1.12 p.m. service from Four Oaks which the early turn Junior Porters living in Sutton Coldfield caught to go home, was the variety of running in locos used as motive power with the 3 coach non-corridor train. I recall Stanier Class 5s, "Patriot" 5XP and 6P, "Jubilee" 5XP and 6P and on one occasion a "Royal Scot" 6P.

SUTTON COLDFIELD LINE PASSENGER MOTIVE POWER

John Tidmarsh the author of an article on "The Sutton Miniature Railway" in Model and Miniature Railways, and once a LMR driver, now based at BRB HQ in London, lived by the Birmingham-Sutton Coldfield line for many years. He advised me of the type of locos that worked on the line in the 1950's. Some of them are seen illustrated throughout the book.

PASSENGER SERVICES

2-6-4T Stanier/Fairbairn were the most common
2-6-2T Fowler
4-4-0 Midland 2P, particularly on the through service to Burton/Derby
2-6-2T Ivatt, on the pull-push services that began a year or so before the March 1956 DMU introduced service.

FREIGHT SERVICES

From John's vantage point he observed the following freight activity:
0-6-0 Class 2, 3, 4 Midland Railway
0-8-0 L.N.W.R.
4-6-0 Class 5
He also remembers with affection a LNWR class 2 0-6-0 cauliflower operating on the line. Three were shedded at Aston for a time: 25848/58/86, and 2 at Walsall: 28594/7.

A.38 ROAD BRIDGE

It was an evocative experience for local and visiting steam enthusiasts to see, hear and smell the passing locos on the northbound coal empty trains as they come up to 1 in 100 incline from Sutton Coldfield surprising passing A.38 motorists as the smoke shot up either side of the Four Oaks road bridge. The 2-8-0 Stanier 8F machines were my favourite, as they stormed the bank going for the brief level respite where Butlers Lane station was opened on 30th September, 1957. Incidentally, Rex Christiansen the author of "The West Midlands — Volume 7" in the David S. Charles regional railway histories of Great Britain told me that, "it was the first half opened in the Birmingham area since 1940". During my time at Four Oaks the Bristol civil engineering firm of Nott Brodie strengthened the bridge and some of the staff used a residential caravan parked in the car park which separated the downside buildings from the 4 station cottages. The severity of the incline in Four Oaks yard was emphasised to me by relief Foreman Billy Hart because staff had to ensure every wagon's brake was firmly on, otherwise the vehicle would naturally run away towards the main line.

WOMEN'S PAINTING GANG

The afternoon Junior Porter had his meal break between 3-4 p.m. when things were generally quiet. I recall an incident when the ladies' painting gang from Walsall was working at Four Oaks. One afternoon they were mucking around in and out of the small foreman's cabin preventing me from cooking my beans to go with the bread and butter. Taking exception to their ribald behaviour and language I left them to get on with it and went back to work. Shortly afterwards the spokeswoman located me working in one of the station rooms and kindly offered to cook my meal, as the other women had started work again.

Retired Four Oaks passenger guard and relief station foreman Billy Hart and his wife *(John Bassett)*

DOG'S HIND LEG

In my first year at Four Oaks, the station's prize possession was the plaque on the down platform building proudly displaying to staff and the public that it had won the 1949 Best Kept Station competition in the Birmingham division. Freres

Bristol based 44746 with Caprotti Valve gear on a diversion passing the Four Oaks station gardens in 1949 *(W.A. Camwell)*

in the Sutton Coldfield News Town Talk in March, 1950 commented that Four Oaks had been selected as the cleanest station with the most trim garden in the Western Section of the Line competition. Mr. Shallis received the trophy. "Among those responsible for the pleasing garden layout was Foreman A.J. Webb who had been at Four Oaks for 17 years. The station had been visited 3 times in the last year. Four Oaks had been placed second in an earlier entry". Regrettably I was partially to blame in seeing us eliminated from the reckoning for any prize in the 1950 contest. Whilst whitewashing the platform edge was called "a dog's hindleg" by some colleagues who of course never volunteered to do it themselves. Some weeks later Mr. Shallis passed on a message to me from the Divisional Passenger Manager, Mr. J.B. Dunkley, after the contest visist. "Tell him to pull his socks up" was the high level command. Gradually we moved up the placings again but I never forget my letting the side down.

PUBLIC SCHOOL LUGGAGE

Not long after the late turn foreman came on duty the three BR lorries brought in parcels not delivered and those for despatch. Mr. Shallis remembered, "that agricultural sprays and equipment went from the Four Oaks Spray Co. and kitchenware from Edward Gill. At the beginning of public school terms we received 20-30 trunks and boxes to go to Repton, Cheltenham and Scottish destinations, from homes on the Four Oaks Estate such as Luttrell Road, Oaklands and Hartopp Road".

LUGGAGE IN ADVANCE

In the summer of 1952 rail passengers, such as public school children in Great Britain could send their luggage in advance. Collection and delivery or conveyance and delivery was 2/2 (11p) and twice the amount for collection, conveyance and delivery. Third class passengers were allowed up to 100 lbs and first class travellers up to 150 lbs.

EARLY PEAK EVENING SERVICES

The evening express service from Birmingham at 5.15 p.m. balanced the morning 8.18 a.m. from Four Oaks but ran non-stop from the city to Wylde Green, arriving at our station at 5.30, with further Monday-Friday evening peak arrivals at 5.56 and the 6.18 which terminated at our station. If my memory serves me correctly, as the vast majority of passengers had tickets, we did not have many excess tickets to issue. But those without a ticket had to wait until the ticket holders had gone through. In between the trains the Junior and Foreman would record any received parcels onto the delivery sheet for the next working day, and the Junior despatched the outgoing parcel traffic.

PASSENGER CENSUS

Since returning to the Midlands as the Chaplain I have met Stanier House staff at the LMR HQ in Birmingham taking part in various Census data collection. I sometimes wonder what the Divisional HQ made of the passenger arrival/departure figures for Four Oaks Station. My Foreman Mr. Webb, regularly "cooked the figures", adding phantom passengers as and when he thought a train needed it. Presumably the Four Oaks figures did not correspond with those of other stations, unless Alf was practising a Branch technique! A further task for the Junior before he left, in my case on the 7.16 p.m., was to prepare the fires ready for lighting by the opposite turn Junior next morning. Another two fires we helped to keep going were those by the water columns to prevent them freezing up in cold weather, so the steam locos could fill up.

THE SIGNAL BOX

The building at Four Oaks which has probably changed the least externally from 1950 is the Signal Box. I enjoyed some

Modern and ancient equipment in the Four Oaks box (*John Bassett*)

happy times there, though by going to sleep after the morning rush on a few occasions it resulted in my getting more work to do! Since our return to the West Midlands I have visited the signalbox finding the outside similar to the 50's. But inside there are some examples of modern electrical/computer equipment to deal with a regular interval service. The March 1985 print from a slide shows signalman Gilbert observing the diagram with some of the modern and ancient technology around him. The box at Four Oaks is now responsible for movements south of Wylde Green to north of Blake Street. Once I was in the box in 1987 when William Gilbert who has now retired, pointed out to me where his Ganger father's railway allotment had been situated near the beginning of the upside sidings. There was a spring near the PW hut. Excess water ran down the culvert on the right of the picture.

A view of Four Oaks with Ganger Gilbert's allotment and hut, top right hand corner (*George Stephens*)

Chapter Three

Coronation and Conscription

After three years as a Junior Porter at Four Oaks I was 18 and no longer a junior! I did some relief work at Blake Street and Alrewas passenger stations before starting my two years national service in the Royal Engineers from August 1953.

BLAKE STREET

This station had wooden plank platforms with combined brick and wooden building structures both sides. As the platforms were on the low side, portable steps were provided on the up and down platforms. The lighting at the time when I was relieving was oil as seen in Mr. Russell's photograph. A heavy cycle with a front parcel rack was kept at the station to enable staff to deliver packages to outlying farms and businesses. Blake Street in 1953 was right out in the country and part of Staffordshire. It had 10 services each day on a weekday. The first up train to Birmingham was the 6.38 a.m. arriving in New Street at 7.20. Folk who wanted to be in Birmingham before 8 a.m. and travel by train had to go down to Four Oaks for the 7.10 service. The first train on the down left at 7.04 arriving at Lichfield City at 7.17. The ex-Brownhills train gave a connection at the City, arriving at T.V. at 7.43 a.m. Blake Street Signal Box was open as required between 6.45 a.m. and 10 p.m. on weekdays.

ALREWAS

The same service was the first weekday morning train to Alrewas arriving at 7.59, called at Barton and Walton seven minutes later, with arrival at Burton-on-Trent at 8.15 a.m. There were seven weekday trains to Burton and six to Lichfield City. Alrewas station was close to the village, although it was separated by the A.38. I recall having to look up the fares book one day for some privilege ticket requests. Similar to Blake Street, Alrewas was in the country. The crossing on the Tamworth Road could be busy. Years later, I visit the signal box regularly. However, since the Tamworth Road had been re-routed, very limited traffic now uses the crossing, but like the 1950's the box is open continuously during weekdays and generally closed at weekends except for diversions and maintenance engineering work.

WHAT'S IN A NAME

In passing, the name of Wichnor Junction where the Walsall via Lichfield, Birmingham via Sutton Coldfield and Lichfield TV Junction services joined the Midland main line, has changed over the last 30 years or so to Wychnor Junction. Gerald Carey, a retired Head of Geography at the John Taylor High School, Barton-under-Needwood advised me that he was not aware of any official local authority decision to change the spelling. He assumes that the, "name was changed by a map maker". However, according to gravestone wording in Wychnor church cemetery both spellings have been used over the years. Mr. Carey's collection of local maps go back to the 1800's. He is interested in the historical aspects of geography.

Blake Street station with low platforms, portable steps and oil lamps in March, 1956. Two days later the new DMU service was introduced on the line (E.S. Russell)

CORONATION DAY 1953

Whilst waiting to be called up in 1953, we had the Coronation of Queen Elizabeth the Second on Tuesday, June 2nd. My rail journeying to Alrewas included a stop at Lichfield TV High Level. At times the West Coast main line traffic could be heard hurtling through the Low Level station. As a gesture of love and respect for the new Queen, Mr. Vic Cowlishaw a Senior Porter at TV Station helped to design the Coronation Garden on the London-bound side of the Low Level station. That 1953 garden may be brought back to mind by some current travellers as they saw a MSC funded scheme taking shape at a similar location in 1986/88. In the spring of 1990 the gardens still appeared unfinished.

Retired Lichfield TV and later City station Master, Bill Ramm, loaned me the photograph showing the maltings at the rear of the Low Level station, reached from the A.38 (now A.5127), the incline marker on the connecting line to Lichfield TV Junction, then onto Alrewas, Wichnor Junction and Burton-on-Trent. Senior Porter Vic Cowlishaw is seen working behind the main display of the Coronation Garden. A comparative view of the Coronation Garden-to-be site is given in E.R. Morten's view shortly before WW II with streamlined 6225 "Duchess of Gloucester" rushing past in the down mainline with the "Royal Scot".

Having mentioned the Lichfield TV Junction, the signal box of that name is featured on page 149 of The Signal Box by the Signalling Study Group who include Shirley relief signalman

Reg Instone, and published by OPC. A further E.R. Morten print shows the TV Junction box in the background with a former Midland 0-6-0 3F pulling away past the waiting 2-8-0 8F engine.

Lichfield TV Low Level Coronation Garden *(Bill Ramm)*

6225 passing the Coronation Garden-to-be site *(E.R. Morten)*

Mr. Ramm's wife, Helen, initiated a significant local community rail activity during the preparations for the 1953 Coronation, by organising two railway outings from Trent Valley area station to see the Coronation's decorations in London. The outings included a 3-hour coach tour in the capital to see the preparation for the big day. After the tour, supper was available at an Oxford Street Restaurant for a further 5/3d on top of the train/coach fare of 22/-. Mrs. Ramm's railway outings became very popular, continuing until shortly before she died in 1986.

NATIONAL SERVICE

At my request Mr. Shallis wrote a letter to the Army authorities requesting a position for me in the Railway Transport Unit at Longmoor Military Railway, in Hampshire. The Army decided I was more cut out to drive lorries than fire steam engines or work on the PW. After basic training, for most of my two years I was attached to a small Royal Engineers unit at Hoo in Kent, about two miles from an isolated South Eastern and Chatham station called Sharnal Street, on the Gravesend central to Allhallows-on-Sea line, 5½ miles from the Thames Estuary resort. The Army service gave me an insight into the Birmingham Snow Hill-Paddington and Birmingham New Street-Euston services. From either London termini I went to a Southern Region station to travel on to Kent. Sometimes on a Sunday, the selected service left Snow Hill at 6.35 p.m. reaching the GWR terminus at 9.20 p.m., or I returned to camp on the overnight 11.45 p.m. from New Street. From Euston, with other servicemen we went by taxi to Holborn Viaduct to proceed on the 2.55 a.m. paper train, alighting at Strood around 4.12 a.m. Alternatively one could go to Gravesend and catch the 5.14 a.m. being at Sharnal Street for 5.35 a.m. Whichever overnight service I used, my workrate on the Monday was poor. When our Unit was working at Chattenden, I saw the Chattenden and Upnor Railway trains. Some of the narrow gauge stock was subsequently sold to the Welshpool and Llanfair Light Railway. Details of the Chattenden and Upnor railway, the Chattenden Haven Tramway and information on "The Isle of Grain Railways" is in the book of that title by Adrain Gray, Oakwood Press, 1974.

Whilst at Hoo, another place we often visited was the Royal Engineers installation at Upnor Hard on the River Medway. It was from Upnor one afternoon with a number of other sappers from our Unit under the direction of our young national service second lieutenant we sallied forth sea bound on a line of khaki-coloured pontoons. Looking back now, it was a

Lichfield TV Junction signal box in the background with a 3F passing an 8F *(E.R. Morten)*

foolhardy expedition, particularly for a non-swimmer like me. A combination of reasons worked against our progress towards the sea, eventually resulting in the officer having to beach the flotilla just short of the point where the Medway joins the mighty Thames. If the skipper had taken us into the estuary we may have needed rescuing, so his decision to cut his losses probably saved lives. Most of my mates moaned about the cold, miserable and muddy conditions we found ourselves in as the pontoons had to be anchored securely on the Kent Island. To my delight, I thought the second lieutenant had made an excellent choice of beaching because the pier he had brought us to looked very much like a railway property. Later investigation revealed we had moored at the former Hundred of Hoo Railway's Port Victoria pier with nearby Port Victoria Hotel. Adrian Gray tells his readers on page 27 of his book, that "because of their frequent use of the Isle of Grain terminal, Edward VII, Queen Alexandra and Kaiser Wilhelm II all contributed funds for the restoration of St. James' Church at Grain village in 1904".

CONFRONTATION WITH THE SERGEANT MAJOR

Being in the forces helped me appreciate the love and kindness shown to me by my parents which I had previously taken for granted. The forces life also made me depend more on my frail christian faith. A verse in Joshua 1:9 from the Covenanter group at Duke Street Hall, Sutton Coldfield, was a support to me on countless occasions: "Have I not commanded you? Be strong and courageous. Do not be terrified; do not be discouraged, for the Lord your God will be with you wherever you go". There were two occasions when I was terrified by our Sergeant Major at the Hoo RE camp. One lunchtime a few of us in our wooden billet were resting on our beds listening to the hired radio when the door was opened and in walked the tall, upright and austere figure of the Unit's Sergeant Major. His intense gaze focusing on each sapper in turn made us all feel guilty and vulnerable to whatever statement he would make. Making the most of his perfect timing, he smiled compassionately asking, "Have we any sport-loving soldiers in this room?" I was too terrified even to move an arm as four other sappers did. On reflection, as the selected four cheerfully went off to report to the S.M. it seemed I had made a mistake in missing out on an enjoyable afternoon's activity provided by a formerly misjudged charitable S.M. During tea I enquired from one of the volunteers who looked exhausted from the afternoon, "what games did the sergeant major let you play?" "Games", was the angry response, "we played no games. He had us two at a time rolling the cricket pitch with the large roller!" A further unexpected meeting with the immaculately-turned out sergeant major was when I answered an order by my sergeant to "go and see the Sergeant Major, pronto. He's asking for you, Bassett". After a quick polish of my work boots, and trying to get the beret badge over my right eye as he frequently informed me it should be, I knocked on his door. Waiting for the "come in", all the recent mishaps I had been involved with were portrayed in my mind like a list of credits at the end of a film or video. One or two of the most serious came back for a second appearance. So my mind looked for excuses why the incidents had happened. "Come in" came the bold order. Approaching his table he said, "Bassett, is it right you have a Bible with you on this camp?" My thinking found it hard to make sense of this question because I did not realise

Lichfield TV staff with Best Kept Gardens Shield *(BR)*

it was an offence to keep the Scriptures on a forces establishment. Another negative thought that came to be was "Who told him?" Once it was confirmed I did possess such a potentially life-changing library of books on the camp, he further startled me with a request "could the CO borrow it for a court-martial, as it appears you have the only Bible in this camp, and he needs one for the defendant to swear on".

LICHFIELD'S NOTABLE DOUBLE

Whilst serving Queen and country, Lichfield gained a notable double in the 1954 Best Kept Gardens Competition with Trent valley winning the Rugby area contest and Lichfield City the one for stations in the Birmingham area. The BR print loaned by Bill Ramm pictures Del Pritchard (booking clerk, who worked with me at Four Oaks, now at Bescot); Ticket Collector Billy Hill; Senior Porter Jack Haire; Senior Porter Vic Cowlishaw; Bill as TV Station Master; and Junior Porter Tony Allport.

NCO's DEMISE

As bonfire night approached in 1954, an extremely smart looking effigy was seen placed with the camp wood, ready for burning. Whether some of the lesser NCO's had made or encouraged others to make the realistic dummy I never found out, but it was abundantly clear who it represented. If asked I would have thought the man concerned could live such an insult and probably make the perpetrators suffer later. However, the NCO concerned was not made of such bold stuff as was revealed on the morning parade of bonfire night. To the sappers' amazement, and probably some NCO's and officers, the Sergeant Major had shaved off his distinctive military-styled moustache so he could not be confused with the bonfire figure!

Chapter Four

January 1955 rail disaster

Less than 7 months from my demob date I was at home for a weekend leave. Walking down the Parade after a Bible Class meeting at Duke Street hall that late Sunday afternoon on January 23rd, 1955, I became aware of a number of ambulances rushing down the A.38 towards Sutton Coldfield Hospital and Birmingham. Shortly afterwards with many other members of the public, I stood behind the railings at the south end (Signalbox end) of the platform as in the Birmingham Gazette aerial view of the disaster.

The York-Bristol nameboards remained intact but we looked at the tragic scene of the diverted express thrown all over the up and down lines in Sutton Coldfield station. Further insights into the tragedy are recorded in photographs by Sutton Coldfield businessman John Hicks, taken over a number of days following the incident.

OTHER PUBLISHED ACCOUNTS OF THE DISASTER

Rex Christiansen in Volume 7 "West Midlands" of the David and Charles Regional History of the Railways of Great Britain states, "Sutton Coldfield was the scene of a spectacular accident in 1955 when a York-Bristol express, diverted because of Sunday working, took the curve through the LNWR station at about twice the 30 mph limit. The death toll was seventeen".

A longer description is given by L.T.C. Rolt in another D and C book Red for Danger. "One of the most inexplicable excessive speed derailments occurred on Sunday, January 23rd, 1955 at Sutton Coldfield, when the 12.15 p.m. York-Bristol express, diverted from its normal route because of engineering works, took the 30 mph curve through the station at between 50 and 60 mph. The Class 5 4-6-0 overturned and the train piled into confusion with the seventeen passengers and enginemen killed and twenty-three injured. A conductor driver who knew the route well was at the controls but the booked driver, who did not know the line, rode in the train. For this he was criticised by Lieut. Colonel Wilson, who nevertheless, could not explain the lapse by the conductor driver".

Aerial view of the disaster *(Birmingham Gazette)*

Mishap locomotive Stanier Class 5 45274 rests on the down platform. The Potteries bus in the goods yard indicates the distances rail staff had to travel *(John Hicks)*

This photograph shows the aged stock used in the breakdown trains *(John Hicks)*

The tragic sight of the diverted 12.15 p.m. York-Bristol which had come to grief in Sutton Coldfield station on Sunday, January 23rd, 1955 *(John Hicks)*

LIBRARY RECORDS OF THE TRAGEDY

The official report on the derailment which occurred that Sunday in January, 1955, and already referred to by L.T.C. Rolt, published by "HMSO 1955 on June 10th, 1955" is available in the Sutton Coldfield Local History Library, plus a considerable number of newscuttings of that event, and subsequent railway related items.

EYE WITNESS ACCOUNTS

Rather than spend time quoting long sections from the comprehensive report by Lt. Col. G.R.W. Wilson and commenting on the informative drawings and plans, I shall relate the views of rail personnel who were involved in the mishap in some way. Space, however, will be given to considering and quoting a little known additional report on the accident.

With a police and fire service presence, the clearing up continues *(Ted Higgs)*

The mark along the platform edging shows where the locomotive jumped the lines and hit the platform *(John Hicks)*

A steam crane lifts one of the vulnerable and frail wooden coaches *(John Hicks)*

COMPLEMENTARY REPORT

Research workers will be aware of the satisfaction that they receive when one of their hunches comes up, although as in this case, the content of the material is about a sad tragedy. I am grateful to retired Police Inspector W.H. Court for his initiative at the time of the police move to their current premises on Lichfield Road. He decided to keep a copy of the Force's Sutton Coldfield Railway Accident Report, "for future reference by historians or anyone else who may be interested".

In 1955 the Sutton Coldfield Police Station was 50 yards from the Railway Station in Station Street. The official Warwickshire police report shows the speed with which the various services provided assistance. The report explains, "The noise of the accident was heard by the Officers on duty who all at once ran to the Railway Station. Superintendent J.C. Gardner and Inspector F. Quinton had a quick look round. Superintendent Gardner returned to the Police Station to summon assistance and the services of ambulances and the Fire Brigade, etc., and Inspector Quinton remained at the Railway Station to organise rescue work, etc.".

The horrific sight at Sutton Coldfield came back to me again 31 years later when I attended the Colwich mishap as the Railway Chaplain in the Midlands in September, 1986, but on the Staffordshire occasion even more folk were involved but only one person died. Many non-Christian rail staff and media spoke of a miracle from God happening at Colwich, though just recognition was given to the vastly improved passenger stock design and production those 30+ years later.

STAFF BRAVERY

In both Lt. Col. Wilson's and Supt. J.C. Gardner's reports, reference is made to train ticket collector G.A. Attenborough. Arthur, in more recent years a chargehand at Lichfield City until his death in April, 1987, shared some of his recollections from the mishap with me. "I was travelling with the late Frank

A front view of one of the cranes at work, with staff looking on *(John Hicks)*

Arthur Attenborough mentioned in both reports for his assistance in stopping a 2-train crash (BR)

Harrison, the train's guard on the 10 coach train, to book on duty at Birmingham then collect tickets on the same train from New Street. As the driver was coming over Bishop Vesey fields, the guard and I thought the driver was approaching the tunnel too fast, so the guard made a short three second brake application to attract the driver's attention. I heard the air intake into the brake valve as the brake was applied". At the rate the train went into the tunnel Arthur "did not envisage an accident but expected the train to lurch". Item 73 of the Lt. Col.'s report states, referring to guard Harrison, "He could have prevented the accident or at least lessened its consequences if he had made a full brake application, and it is much to be regretted that he did not have the courage of his convictions . . . Guard Harrison has an excellent service record". Arthur also speaks well of him.

London based John Tidmarsh told me that a "number of folk recalled hearing a piercing locomotive whistle from mishap locomotive Stanier Class 5 45274 at the time of the accident", though it was not mentioned in either report.

According to the police report "the tenth" (rear coach in which Arthur was travelling) "remained on the line with little damage done to it. The rear of the train was some 22 yards outside the mouth of the tunnel on the Lichfield side of the station. Both up and down lines were completely blocked with the track destroyed for some 150 yards". Arthur jumped out when the train stopped, onto the ballast, running up the ramp on the up side (Station Street) platform. There was a wheel barrow. Although it was cold I took off my overcoat, jacket, scarf, cap and flung them on the barrow. I batted up the platform. I didn't notice the things such as sleepers, sleeper chairs, etc., littering the platform. I ran up to the signalbox because I knew the Bristol-York was due. When they were on time they normally passed at Gravelly Hill". The door was open and Derek Smith a locomotive fireman on his way to work was already in the signalbox. Fireman Smith "was thrown out on to the line by the impact, and although dazed and badly shocked, realised an express train was due in the opposite direction. He had run to the signalbox". The police report stated because Fireman Smith "was unable to speak" on the telephone to control, Arthur who "got to the signalbox a few seconds after Smith "simultaneously told" Smith the sequence of signals to push back so the northbound driver

would be given the danger signals from the Wylde Green approach. He also rang the 12 bell code of 3-3-3-3 for an emergency which was called the "roll call". All duty staff who heard that bell would listen in from their boxes". A couple of minutes before, Four Oaks Passenger Guard Billy Hart saw the York bound express crossing the Chester Road railway bridge.

SECOND CRASH AVERTED

According to Arthur Attenborough "the north-bound driver saw that the distant semaphore signal was off going for the first overbridge past Wylde Green Station just 1¼ miles from the accident. But the driver noticed the signal was in the down (danger) position when he was on the other side of the bridge. The train was stopped well clear of the obstruction". The Ministry of Transport and Civil Aviation report said "the northbound express stopped 470 yards from the accident". Press reports put it much closer. The Daily Mirror told its readers, "The driver of Express No. 2 slammed on his brakes, His packed train screamed to a stand-still only 200 yards from the wreck".

It was near this point that the northbound express driver saw that the Sutton Coldfield distant signal had been put back to danger. Many members of the public gave heroic and valuable assistance. Most of the stories can be found in the newscutting files, as well as subsequent accounts on an anniversary of the accident.

Reflecting on what he had done, Arthur told me, "I was given spiritual assistance to complete that task". At the Attenborough family's invitation in 1987 I took part in Arthur's funeral, mentioning his acknowledgement that God helped him in January, 1955.

Sutton Coldfield lengthman Walter Roberts who retired from the railway in 1971 after 41 years' service, thinking back to the accident said "We did whatever we could to help. The engine dome burnt itself out on the flowerbed. The rails were twisted up like wire". The former New Street driver Ted "Buttons" Higgs who kindly donated some of his photos was allowed out in charge of a loco for the first time, when he took a breakdown train to the crash scene.

QUEEN'S CONCERN

The Queen sent a message to the then Transport Minister, Mr. Boyd-Carpenter, saying, "please express my sincere sympathy with the relatives of those who lost their lives and those who were injured".

Lt. Col. Wilson's report advised that during the second test run, just a few days before he was to submit his report, one of the officers on the footplate had to apply the brake to stop the test train from going into the tunnel too fast like the mishap train.

Former Sutton Signalman William Gilbert told me he was at his father's railway terraced home at Four Oaks the crash afternoon when his brother John on duty at Four Oaks rushed over to tell them of the accident. William caught the first bus to Sutton and dad, Ganger Jack Gilbert checked the lines for anything broken to Sutton. William booked on at the Sutton box before 5 p.m. staying there the next 13 hours.

To conclude the focus on the Sutton Coldfield railway accidents here are some selected details of the help provided, noted in Superintendent J.C. Gardner's report of January 31st, 1955.

4.11 p.m.
    Accident occurred

4.19 p.m. (Fire)
    One pump escape and wireless van from Sutton Coldfield fire station arrived. The following had been ordered and were on their way to the scene.

A northbound freight approaching the Sutton Coldfield distant signal *(Richard Thorne)*

1 pump escape from Coleshill
7 fire appliances, 1 equipment van and 1 canteen van from Birmingham.
2 walkie-talkies, 1 wireless car, 1 breakdown van and 2 salvage tenders from Warwick.

4.21 p.m. (Ambulance)
Three ambulances from Sutton Coldfield Depot arrived and personnel took over first aid treatment and conveyance to Sutton Coldfield Hospital, first casualties arriving there at 4.30 p.m.
The following ambulances had been called and arrived as follows:-
13 from Birmingham 4.24-5.14 p.m.
  (12 standing by at Erdington)
2 from Coleshill 4.35 p.m.
3 from Grendon 4.45 p.m.
3 from Solihull 4.50 p.m.

4.25 p.m. (Doctors)
The first doctor arrived and within a quarter of an hour 10 doctors were at the scene. By 5 p.m. six more doctors had arrived with the blood transfusion unit and mobile surgical unit.

5.10 p.m.
Railway police from Birmingham arrived (1 super-intendent, 1 inspector, 1 sergeant and 3 constables)

7.00 p.m.
Approximately 70 police officers were on duty.
Shortly after 7 p.m. when it was known all injured were clear of the train, the railway breakdown gangs commenced clearing the wreckage and some of the police were dismissed. Special constables still arriving.

Monday, January 24th
The first two of the trapped bodies to be recovered from the wreckage of the train were those of the pilot driver and fireman, whose bodies were recovered from the cab of the overturned engine at 6 a.m. The last body was recovered from the wreckage at 11.30 p.m.

Wednesday, January 26th
The H.M. Coroner C.W. Iliffe, Esq., conducted the inquest with a Jury in the Magistrates Court of Sutton Coldfield, on the 17 deceased persons. After evidence of identification and cause of death, H.M. Coroner adjourned the inquest for four weeks.

Normal train services were resumed on the line at 6.10 a.m. that morning, the track and platform having been repaired. There is, however, much debris from the wrecked coaches to be cleared from the sides of the tracks.

The closing words came from Sir Brian Robertson, the then Chairman of the BTC on the evening of the crash "The only impression I came away with, but which I would like to emphasise, is that once the disaster had occurred all the steps that could be taken by anybody to redeem its consequences were, so far as I was able to judge, excellently taken. Police, ambulances, fire brigade, voluntary workers and men of British Railways, all of them showed a presence of mind, initiative and, in many cases, courage which aroused one's admiration".

THIRTY YEAR RE-OPENING

An almost unknown phenomenon that resulted from the Sutton Coldfield (LNWR) — Birmingham train service being curtailed for 3 days was told by now retired Saltley driver Bill Alcock. "We lived at Aldridge during the time of the Sutton Coldfield disaster, and on Monday morning following I travelled to work at Saltley on the first train from Aldridge (about 7 a.m.) and we were surprised to see it stop at the old Sutton Town station, and passengers get on. The following day I was on an earlier turn of duty and we took empty stock from Saltley to Sutton Park and then worked a train (about 7.45 a.m.) to New Street stopping at Sutton Town, Penns etc.". The station had closed in 1925.

SUTTON–LICHFIELD LINE ACCIDENTS

Further fatal accidents have emerged during my research work for Cross City connections, but only one is fairly well known,

occurring on 12th April, 1902. A summary in the local press 50 years later read, "the 9.35 p.m. train from Sutton Coldfield to Birmingham consisted of eight coaches drawn by tank engine No. 32. It left from the bay platform, i.e. the one now used by coaches for the car-sleeper trains. To get on the right track, the train had to run for a short distance along the track used by trains approachng the station from the Birmingham direction. While making the manoeuvre the train collided head-on with the 9.15 a.m. New Street — Four Oaks train, also a eight coach train and hauled by Tank engine No. 751. One lady was killed and 52 people injured. At the subsequent inquiry, it was established that the accident had been caused by the Four Oaks train, overshooting a signal which was at danger. The evidence revealed that the signal was showing a dim light due to a faulty oil lamp".

The Sutton Coldfield News account of the disaster gave an example of how ordinary people had taken to commuting from Sutton to Birmingham to carry out their daily occupations. The fatality, Miss Olyve Mary brown (22) of Lower Queen Street, used a "second class season ticket" and was "employed as a waitress at Mr. treadwell's restaurant, Cannon Street, Birmingham, at a salary of 20s weekly". Miss Brown's father had formerly worked on the LNWR as a signalman.

The newspaper continued, "The injured were at once conveyed to the waiting rooms where a number of medical men of the town had gathered. These include Drs. Evans, Tunstall, Hobbes, Jerome, and Chavasse. Ambulances had been obtained from the Town Hall and the Police Station, so that everything possible was done for the sufferers".

Workmen rebuilding the down platform edging. The upside platform remains out of use *(John Hicks)*

Similar to the more severe crash in 1955, the nearness of the police station enabled officers to be on the scene quickly. "Police-Sergaent Thomas Jackson said that when in Station Street about 9.40 p.m. he heard a crash. He immediately went to the L and NW station where he saw a number of people. He then went down the line, and having ascertained what had happened, the ambulances were sent for".

A further mishap is referred to at the end of the 1902 news account. "It is fifteen or sixteen years since a serious accident of any kind occurred at Sutton station. At that time Sutton was a terminus, and a special train for Four Oaks races ran right into the wall. Happily, no-one was killed".

22 YEARS WAIT

Sutton Coldfield residents wishing to go by train to Lichfield without a detour via Birmingham or Burton from 1862 had to wait until December 15th, 1884 before the Four Oaks extension was opened when "the bells of Shenstone Church rang out a merry peal" and at "various stations there was a reception of artillery in the shape of a number of fog signals". The incident that happened resulting in a man's death is not usually mentioned, about that opening day. Well within the ringing of the Shenstone chimes, 33 year old William Field, of Hollingshaw, Manchester, "was run over while engaged i shunting on the temporary line at the back of the Shenston church, receiving such serious injuries that he died in less tha an hour after. William, a rope runner, attempted to catch hol of the rail of the engine, but missed it, and fell. He was taken from the wheels and carried to the Buck's Head Inn". Othe details included, "The new extension of railway from Sutto Coldfield to Lichfield was opened for passenger traffic o Monday last, having already been used for goods traffic sinc September. The first train left Birmingham at 7.10 a.m. and o its arrival at Sutton the engine was gaily decked with flags an evergreens. A number of local residents proceeded on the firs journey, and were augmented by others at each of the stations On the return to Sutton, which was accomplished shortly ate half past eight o'clock, Mr. Sutton, the General Traffi Manager, and party breakfasted at the Royal Hotel, while supernumeracy party, including the contractor's principl employees and several officials of the company, were also wel entertained at the Station Hotel".

Another fatality was before the extension was open. I happened when Ganger Richard Webster was with his men on Monday, February 3rd, 1879 clearing snow from the line. Mr Webster had helped lay the rails for the contractors when the 1862 line was being constructed, and had 43 years' service or the LNWR when he was instantaneously killed by the engine

With rubble and stock still around, services had restarted. Mr. Shallis is seen walking towards the crossing *(John Hicks)*

at crushed him near Sutton Coldfield signal box during the snow clearing task. A verdict of "Accidental Death" was recorded on Richard Webster and William Field.

The last of the fatalities I have noted took place in 1886, according to John Marshall in his paper, "A Dissenting Society", P.11, Wade Street URC, Lichfield. "In March 1886, Mr. Fred Mumford, a sunday school teacher, 'while in the execution of his duty at Lichfield City station shunting a train . . met with a serious accident by falling in front of some rolling trucks. This was a fortnight after his marriage'". To conclude these sad accounts of railway deaths on the LNWR line we turn to another eye-witness report of the 23rd January 1955, tragedy. Page one of the Sutton Coldfield News, the issue 6 days after the accident reported "Mr. and Mrs. G.W. Overton who live in the old Station Master's house on Sutton Coldfield station, were sitting in their living room when they heard the ill-fated express rumbling through the tunnel. 'We are used to the sound of passing trains', said Mr. Overton, who is a Station Inspector at Birmingham and has worked on the railways for 36 years, 'but this one made a very unusual noise. There was a roar and then silence, which you could cut with a knife'. His daughter Margery rushed to the platform and then told her parents of the crash".

On a front page spread on Friday, May 6th, 1955, Sutton Coldfield News readers were given a preview of the DMU service to start on the New Street–Sutton Coldfield–Lichfield City line, ten months later in March, 1956. The report continued:

"During the demonstration run of the New Street–Castle Bromwich BIF special diesel train on Friday, the editor of the News was assured by an official of British Railways that such trains will be running between Birmingham and Lichfield — and therefore calling at Erdington, Sutton Coldfield and other intermediate stations — early in 1956.

"Starting of the service depends solely on delivery of the rolling stock and training the crews. delivery for the Lichfield service is expected at the end of the summer. The service will have been well run-in for some 18 months, in fact in time for the heavy demands of the 1957 Scout Jamboree in Sutton Park". The journalists commented on the "comfortable seats, smart interior and light weight luggage rack". A photograph of the Midland committee of the 1957 Scout Jamboree was seen on page one of the Sutton Coldfield News of Friday, October 7th, 1955.

Chapter Five

Disaster aftermath

That mishap came back to me from time to time in my last months in the forces. When I returned to the railway in September, 1955, it was as a porter at Sutton Coldfield station. There remained a strange feeling in one of the upside waiting rooms used as a temporary mortuary. One of my jobs was to clean it along with other rooms on the station.

Some of the Sutton Coldfield Station premises remain the same as in 1955 with the exception of the downside bay buildings, goods facilities and signal box.

The choice, competition, building and operation of the eventual Birmingham to Sutton Coldfield railway line is covered in Roger Lea's "Steaming up to Sutton", published by Westwood Press Publications in 1984. Mr. Lea, the Regional Librarian and the Sutton Coldfield Local History Librarian Miss Marion Baxter have both been most helpful, encouraging me in writing Cross City connections.

41223 emerging from Sutton Coldfield tunnel *(Eric S. Russell)*

Signal reflections

Although the box camera photos are not sharp, they can give an insight into the environment around the station in the mid-1950's which is a significant time in this narrative.

The first two photos were taken from the top of the signal on the downside, close to the tunnel entrance as seen in E.S. Russell's view of 41223 emerging from the tunnel on October 1st, 1955.

The first view includes the Station Hotel c1860, the spire of the Congregatational Church, now the United Reformed Church, and the Station Street cottages which have been demolished.

The second view also includes some of the demolished 1860 railway cottages, the 1859 Town Hall which is no longer in use for that purpose and the 1298 Holy Trinity Church.

The third photograph taken from the signal gantry depicted in Senior Porter John Forsythe's shot at 5.30 a.m. some years later of the recently arrived overnight Stirling-Sutton motorail service.

Incidentally the signal to the right is one locomotive fireman Derek Smith put to danger at the instructions of Arthur Attenborough.

Holy Trinity church can be seen in the background and to the right some buildings Mr. Redwood advised me have been demolished. The line of buildings in the centre from right to left show a rear view of the Parade shops. The houses in the foreground which have also been demolished were situated in Avenue Road. The building to the left of the houses was the rear garage of A.T. Hastilow, the removal and coach firm. Miss Bracken's drawing of C.1863 in "Steaming up to Sutton" is from the railway embankment around the same place as this third photograph.

Steaming up to Sutton (John Forsythe)

Top right:
A wet dull Sutton roof top picture (John Bassett)

Middle right:
Part of Sutton Town Centre in 1956 John Bassett)

Bottom right:
The 1298 Holy Trinity Church dominates the Sutton 1956 skyline (John Bassett)

Sutton Coldfield Station Plan

The 1880 Sutton Coldfield station plan used in "Steaming up to Sutton" shows the turntable and I wondered if it is the same piece of equipment taken out by Ganger Sid Dainty of Park Lane and local Lengthmen shown in this photograph of August 10th, 1937, donated by Mr. Walter Roberts (page 34).

John Forsythe on the bay platform (*John Bassett*)

Mr. Roberts remembers the turntable being there when he joined the railways in the 1920's. It was used by engines to run around their trains. Mr. Roberts also recalled that "goods staff used the turntable to manually turn round wagons".

The Fruit Department Manager of Chamberlains, on Sutton Parade, Harold Groves, also recalled the turntable in Sutton Coldfield (LNWR) yard.

Push & Pull

By the time of my returning to the railway, push and pull services had started to operate as seen in this view at Sutton Coldfield of the 6.33 p.m. New Street to Four Oaks on July 27th, 1955, of Monument Lane (3E) tank 41224.

Guard Leslie Eccles told me he remembered the "2 coach push-pull trains running into the Sutton Coldfield bay platform for about 2-4 weeks, then being extended to Four Oaks. The Monument Lane engines used included 41223, 41224 — as seen in the photo — and 41320".

Many of the basic branch line arrangements at Four Oaks applied to Sutton Coldfield, such as parcel services with the three same vehicles, the same daily trippers and many of the

same staff working the trains. However, Sutton Coldfield as one may expect was a more substantial station. It was in a clos position to the Royal Borough's shopping and administrativ centre. Sutton Coldfield's residents made use of th employment, shopping, leisure and transport facilities o Birmingham but remained proud of being in Warwickshire an not part of the City of Birmingham. Sutton was a Royal Tow with a history, including the Park, that it intended to kee outside Brum at any price.

Staffing

The Station Master in the mid 1950's was Mr. McCarter from Wales, like Booking Clerk Agnes Eacott. Mr. McCarter' previous S.M. position was at Colbourne South in Lancashire John Forsythe originated from Ireland, whilst the other staf including Booking Clerk Ken Coleman tended to be mor local. Ken and I had some encouraging talks about th privileges and responsibilities of being Followers of Jesu Christ.

Another stalwart at Sutton Coldfield in the 1950's wa Senior Porter David Higham seen sharing a shunting pole wit van driver Les Shelley on the bay platform. The cycle rack t the left of David was in front of the staff room. The room wa also used by the Roberts Brothers, both Lengthmen, a Firewatchers in WW II.

John Forsythe is seen on the same Bay platform, but furthe down, showing the buffers, some lorry trailers, goods van and the goods shed, which was later demolished in preparatio for the car sleeper services.

David Higham and Les Shelley (*John Bassett*)

Railway staff frequently became local personalities in their own right for a variety of reasons. John on two occasions was used as a model for a group of artists at the Sutton Coldfield College of Art.

In the silhouette photograph with the Class 4F on Tripper 162 at 12.02 p.m. to Shenstone can be seen three Sutton porters in the mid 1950's including George Perryman on the right, at the northern end of platform one (Birmingham departures) on the up line. It was close to this point that Arthur Attenborough threw down some of his outer clothing in a barrow before "batting" down the platform at the 1955 mishap. This spot is near the Booking Office Building on platform one.

Handbook of stations

The 1956 edition of the British Transport Commission Handbook of stations states that Sutton had a 5 ton crane available in the goods side of the business. The station could provide and convey passenger, parcels, and miscellaneous traffic, goods traffic, furniture vans, carriages, motor cars, portable engines, machines on wheels, horse boxes and prize cattle vans and carriages and motor cars by passenger or parcels trains. In comparison, Four Oaks could provide and convey similar services but had no crane.

Freight Facilities

Relating his memories of the goods side of Sutton station, John Forsythe remembers "Tripper 166 usually arrived from Lichfield City about midday leaving for Erdington between 1.30 — 2.00 p.m. with full loads being left for Tripper 162 later in the day". The 1957 times from the working timetable are on page 10.

"The firms we served included: Ernest H. Derricott and Southerns, Martineu and Smith all of Coleshill Street, and

Push and Pull service at Sutton Coldfield (*John Edgington*)

Local lengthmen, August 1937 *(Walter Roberts)*

Alexander Control on the Reddicap Trading Estate. Lever Brothers stored cattle food in the precast concrete building. The goods shed was used for local deliveries. On the coal and coke side, could be seen staff of Comley, Davenport and Smith and Machin. Two other local firms had no offices at the wharf, their wagons came direct from the collieries. Harold Warford was one of those private coal merchants without office facilities on site".

Most of the goods traffic to and from the 216 Maintenance Unit of the RAF at the edge of Falcon Lodge Estate was tyres, aero engines and pumps. A member of the unit is seen resting on the back platform. More recently the site became the Army's St. George's Barracks.

Tripper Reflections

Retired Traction Instructor Ken Beasley and retired colleague Bill Dobson recall "T162 and T166". In their steamdays on the

Silhouette of Sutton staff *(John Bassett)*

Sutton line "T166 was only concerned with freight. Tha means" emphasised Ken, "anything other than coal. Havin shunted all the goods yard, except Chester Road which wa coal only, the crew were relieved at Erdington at 1.45 p.m Erdington was the busiest goods yard on the branch".

Shunting Allowance/Awaiting path

The following amounts of time were allowed to Trippers 16 and 166 according to June 9th to September 14th, 195 working timetable of freight trains:

Mondays — Fridays
   Down line (to Lichfield City)
T162   Erdington 1hr. 23 mins; Sutton Coldfield 57 mins

   Up line (to Birmingham)
T166   Shenstone 10 mins; Four Oaks 59 mins; Sutto Coldfield 47 mins; Erdington 1 hr. 53 mins.

T162   Shenstone 2 hrs. 26 mins; Blake Street 15 mins; Fou Oaks 15 mins; Sutton Coldfield 47 mins; Erdingto 10 mins.

Member of 216 MU RAF camp *(John Forsythe)*

Passenger Parcels

Leaving the goods department "that brings in most money according to David Higham, John Forsythe said that "ther was a good flow of passenger train parcels traffic to Sutton fo firms like BHS, Woolworth, Rayboulds and John Hicks th outfitters. The cream for Plowrights Cafe had to be there in th morning otherwise I had to return it. We had boxes of fish fo MacFisheries".

The Wooden Hill

Parcels traffic was loaded up on a jack barrow or a four whee barrow, then taken up the Wooden Hill for checking anc recording on a driver's delivery sheet.

I often wondered what it sounded like to Railway Inspecto George Overton of New Street station and his family whc occupied a railway house, underneath the Sutton booking office and Woodenhill, when the parcels were drawn up the incline. They could not have had much peace because the Sutton staff were around from 6 a.m. until about 10.30 p.m. each weekday in the early 1950's. The introduction of the frequent time interval diesel multiple units from March, 1956 meant that the Overton family had platform staff around until at least 11.15 p.m.

A view of the woodenhill, with station house below before colour light signalling was installed, looking towards the main booking office (*Lens of Sutton*)

Mr. Thomas in former station master's house (*John Bassett*)

The Lens of Sutton photo shows the wooden hill in relation to the station house below.

Even before the staff booked on, Ken Beasley referred to "A weekdays 4.30 a.m. train from Aston Goods of empty coal wagons through Sutton to Wichnor Sidings", which no doubt disturbed the family. There was possibly more disturbance later in the day on the return trip. "The section between Four Oaks and Wylde Green", continued Ken, "was known as the switchback. Whereas the passenger trains slowed for the Sutton tunnel, the freight tried to keep up the speed to get up the incline to Wylde Green. Different driving techniques were required".

External view of the *Chess* building in 1987 (*John Bassett*)

Chess

Mr. Reg Hollins of Westwood Press informed me that "the accommodation occupied by Mr. and Mrs. Overton and their two daughters was taken over by *Chess* Magazine in November, 1960. The late Mr. B.H. Wood, OBE, owner and editor of *Chess*, set up his own printing works and office here for his international Chess business, which he ran until shortly before his death in April, 1989. It was in recognition of Mr. B.H. Wood, an internationally known Chess Master, that the Chess theme was used to name the courts of the Gracechurch Centre when it opened in 1974".

During my Spring, 1987 revisit to that part of Sutton Coldfield station I met Alan Thomas who joined *Chess* at the present location in 1968. Mr. Thomas is seen working; in a room of the former Station Master's house.

Mr. Thomas confirmed that the staff in the *Chess* buildings could clearly hear folk using the incline. When I called again in 1989, *Chess* had been part of the Pergamon Press group since August, 1987.

Chapter Six

DMUs long reign

At the end of February 1956 "the diesel train service between Birmingham New Street and Lichfield City calling at Sutton Coldfield and intermediate stations was given a trial civic run" so reported the Sutton Coldfield News. "The Royal Town" it continued, "was represented by its Mayor (Counc. H.H. Turner) and the train waited for several minutes in Sutton Coldfield station where several townspeople had gathered specially to see it".

Mr. J.W. Watkins, the General Manager, London Midland Region, Midland Area, later said at a reception referring to DMUs "this was part of the British Railways modernisation plans" but he stressed the "difficulty of rolling stock supply. The new service would relieve road congestion and bring money to BR coffers".

A photograph by Mr. Spencer records the first public Birmingham New Street to Lichfield DMU service on arrival at the City station, on Monday, March 5th, 1956, being the 6.30 a.m. from New Street. Mr. Spencer's copy of the white and blue 'New Diesel Services' leaflet introducing the DMU trains between March 5th to June 10th gives 35 weekly services on the down with 36 on the up, and 8 and 7 respectively on Sundays. Out of the off-peak period the trains left New Street on the hour up to Four Oaks, and the half hour continuing up to Lichfield City.

The Cheap Day Return fares were shown as Birmingham New Street to: Vauxhall and Duddeston -/6; Aston -/8; Gravelly Hill -/9; Erdington -/12; Chester Road 1/-; Wylde Green 1/2; Sutton Coldfield 1/4; Four Oaks 1/7; Blake Street

First public DMU service from New Street to Lichfield City (*Arthur Spencer*)

One of the new diesel multiple units at Four Oaks at the end of the first week in local public service *(Eric S. Russell)*

1/11; Shenstone 2/5; Lichfield City 2/11. Car parking facilities in the Spring of 1956 were only "available at Sutton Coldfield, Four Oaks and Blake Street passenger stations", according to the leaflet.

Echoes of the day tripper tickets on WMPTE services come to mind as Mr. Spencer talks of the availability of LMS tickets on the former LNWR and Midland lines through Sutton in 1937. "A few Day Return tickets had the return usable on the 'Midland Red', after the war for a while Day Returns were available on any train. By 1964 New Street to Four Oaks Day Returns were only available after 9.30 a.m. Monday-Fridays". In the 1937 timetable and fares leaflet railway passengers were advised "The return halves of these tickets are available to return by the Midland 'Red' Omnibus (excepting Service No. 105 via Walmley and No. 107 via New Oscott). Midland 'Red' ordinary tickets between the same points will be valid to return by rail".

Passenger adaptation

I recall that Management and staff were apprehensive about how long it would take to load the new DMUs as the public had nine doors or so a side with non-corridor carriages to get into, while the new stock had two. We need not have worried, the public quickly adapted to the smart new, cleaner green trains. To publicize the new intensive DMU service, timetables were put through all doors in the Sutton Coldfield areas, that were reasonably near to a station. Rail staff were paid to deliver the timetables.

My photograph taken in the upside sidings on the line nearest the upside bank at Four Oaks shows four guards in front of the new DMUs. I am not sure whether this was before or after the trains were in public service. A number of rail people have identified these guards except the man, second from the left. L to R, Harold Fitzmaurice (Curzon St.), third from left Tom Rain (Curzon St) and New Street Guard, George Reed.

Driver Vacancies

Ken Beasley was one of a number who went from Saltley to take up the 21 DMU driver vacancies at Monument Lane on February 13th, 1956. The vacancies had been created by the introduction of the new services.

West Midland guards in front of new DMU stock in Four Oaks upside siding (*John Bassett*)

"Spectacular Increase"

Rex Christiansen wrote "The suburbs between Birmingham and Sutton Coldfield are fashionable, well populated areas, and when the line was dieselised in 1956, the attraction of the new trains brought a spectacular increase in annual passenger returns, which rose from about 75,000 to 2,500,000 in two years".

Researchers in the 1990's can observe an even more frequent service on the Sutton Coldfield section of the cross-city line, with the 15 minute interval timetable that began in May, 1989. Electrification between Redditch and Lichfield TV HL will see the maximising of the line's passenger carrying potential. Such higher loadings must lead to the eventual re-opening of the Lichfield via Alrewas line to passenger trains onto Burton and Derby.

The earlier potential financial possibilities of the Four Oaks line was shown with the reintroduction of trains in May 1987 on Sundays to Butlers Lane, Blake Street, Shenstone and Lichfield City.

The 1950's increase in passengers was reflected on spring and summer bank holiday weekends when thousands from Birmingham and the Black Country descended on Sutton Coldfield station to visit the lovely Sutton Park. Around six or so extra ticket barrier staff were allocated per shift to deal with the influx of passengers on the Mondays. However, on the Bank holiday Tuesdays which still attracted many folk, the local staff had to do their best, without help.

Regular tasks

John Forsythe could be seen at regular intervals with a bag hanging from his shoulders as he went over to the south end of the Station Street buildings on the up platform. He would be hidden for some moments then reappear on top of the water tank seen in E.S. Russell's view of June 20th, 1949. This photograph also shows the curvature of the platform valencing, as it was prior to the crash. John's task was to drop softwater blocks into the tank.

Another regular job was that of keeping the signal lamps clean and bright. This was one of my tasks which took quite a while. Having brought them in, they were serviced and returned for a further week. The most scary one to me was the Sutton home signal on the Four Oaks approach into the tunnel. The signal itself was high but the deep cutting appeared to accentuate the height. I was thankful many times for the safe recesses cut into the side of the tunnel at intervals so duty folk like me could get out of the way of trains as they came through. Similar to the gantry in John Forsythe's picture the Sutton home signals really jumped around if you happened to be attending them when the "Bobby" pulled off the "peg".

Tunnel Length?

My research has uncovered three different official lengths for the Sutton Coldfield tunnel, they are:

(a) 173 yards, shown in a route and gradient plan from LMR HQ in 1983. The document is probably late 1940's/early 1950's though Butlers Lane has been added later.

(b) The second measurement of 172 yards is on the Four Oaks Signal box diagram, noted in March, 1987, and the third distance of

(c) 171 yards, is stated in the Ministry of Transport and Civil Aviation Railway accident report by Lt. Col. G.R.S. Wilson, referred to a number of times.

John Forsythe was seen at regular intervals on the top of this tank (*Eric S. Russell*)

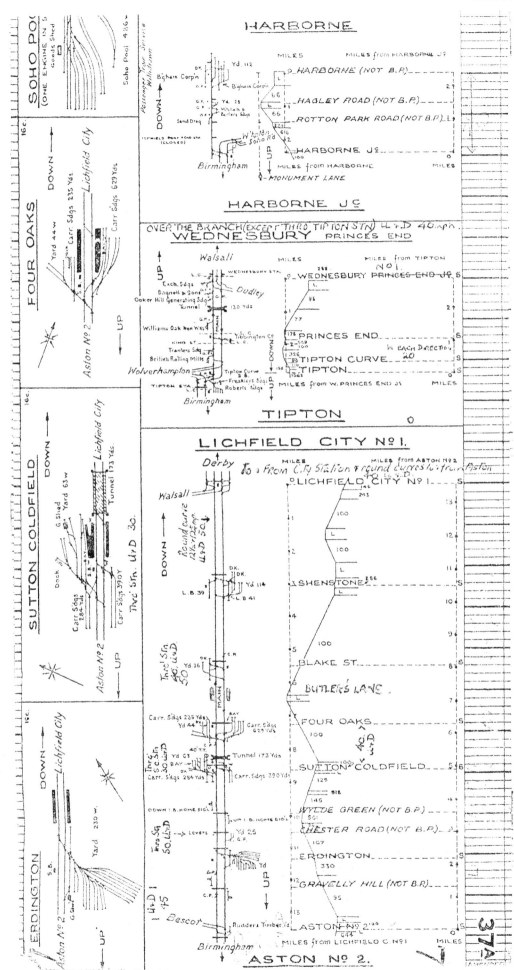

1940/1950s gradient plan *(British Rail)*

Trackman Walter Roberts, carrying out another miscellaneous duty (*John Bassett*)

The same distance of 171 yards is given in the Hendrys' book. Responding to my query about the tunnel measurement, R. Powell Hendry says "It is in fact depressingly common to find that there are several different "official" lengths for structures such as bridges and tunnels, unlike locomotives where a 1″ discrepancy will be pounced upon by an army of readers, the limited numbers of people interested in tunnels, etc., makes certainty difficult, particularly as the length can truly vary, depending upon how it is calculated. With bridges it is especially troublesome, as clear span, centreline of abutments, length of girders, etc., can all be taken, with tunnels there are similar subtle variations . . . perhaps 6 feet for Sutton tunnel is not too bad, though it *is* infuriating. With Sutton, the difference could be centre line length or max. length as the curve will affect these".

The current official length is taken from the British Rail Southern Section — Sectional appendix of February 1975, shown to me by train crew leader John Williams: "Sutton Coldfield tunnel is 172 yards". However, just to complicate it again, the London Midland Area and Regional bridge cards state the official length is 171 yards! One BR engineer thought the three measurements were arrived at by (a) measuring along one wall (b) down the centre of the tunnel and (c) along the other tunnel wall.

P W duties

The permanent way gang members in the 1950's could be seen on weekdays walking the length to make sure the track was in a satisfactory state to receive traffic. Mr. Walter Roberts told me that he and fellow trackmen could be called out in poor weather to be of assistance to Signalman Gilbert or Weston. The Trackman received 3/6 (17½p) for snow sweeping or fogworking. If a train had to be stopped, Walter placed three

The annual presentation of safety awards to Sutton Coldfield BR drivers (*British Rail*)

DMUs long reign 41

hots (detonators) near the signal post then the other three up to a mile away. "A driver hearing three will be prepared for danger. If he goes over another three, he will stop", commented Mr. Roberts.

Lorry drivers

Reference has been made a number of times to the BR Lorry Drivers based at Sutton Coldfield and they are seen at the annual presentation of safety awards. The photo includes third from left Driver Harry Bennett, fifth from left, Sutton Coldfield Foreman Tom Perks, next to Driver Les Shelley, then Station Master at the time, Mr. J.D. Childs, and far right, Driver Alf Archer.

As we come to a close of Sutton Coldfield LNWR station four more photographs of John Hicks are included. 44490 on a passenger service showing the downside valencing before the accident date, and wagons, trucks in the goods yard.

44490 on passenger service (*John Hicks*)

Moving further along the same platform pre-accident days, 40125 is in charge of a 3-coach local (*John Hicks*)

A brief visit to the upside to watch 41224 taking water (*John Hicks*)

44145 almost clouds the Sutton box out of view as it moved the freight towards the tunnel. Some goods traffic can be seen in the yard (*John Hicks*)

Chapter Seven

Birmingham steam scenes

Eventually I applied for promotion, moving in 1956 to New Street as a left luggage Clerk/Lost Property Officer. I seem to remember that there was an office on platform one on the LNWR side and an office on the MR side. Although I had gone into New Street many times, the two sides of the old railways had not forcefully came to me before. The independent organisation of the two companies of the London and North Western and the Midland had stopped in 1923, but their distinctive presence was still there in 1956.

Part of the LNW side is seen in John Hick's views firstly of 42616 at New Street on a local service to Four Oaks.

The second print in the LNWR area is 4-4-0 2P 40511 near 2-6-2T 3P 40073.

The following two photographs seek to capture the atmospheric side of the Midland with its gloomy over all roof.

In 1958 there was about 370 trains a day using New Street station. The evenings could be very quiet at times.

My present Railway Chaplain office on Platform 1B from where I seek to share a Christian perspective in the local Railway industry is about 300 yards from one of the left luggage offices I worked in. In terms of the World's rat race my progress of 300 yards in 30 years may take some beating!

Out and about

One of the most enjoyable periods of my life in BR employment was from April-August, 1957 when I was promoted to a temporary relief travelling ticket collector position working from New Street. After two weeks training

The L.N.W.R. side of New Street station (*John Hicks*)

A double headed holiday express leaving the Midland site of New Street station amid much smoke and steam (*John Bassett*)

on the trains by a number of collectors I worked on passenger services to Derby, Sheffield, Leeds, Coventry, Euston, Bristol, Crewe and Wolverhampton. I was offered 2/- (10p) by a passenger on the Stour Valley service, which I politely refused. He was a member of a card sharping team that operated on the Birmingham-Wolverhampton trains, assisting unsuspecting travellers to lose their money through set-up games of cards. When I asked rail staff at Wolverhampton (HL) to take action, no-one would get involved. Eventually a warning was given over the station's public address system.

GWR Snow Hill

Whilst thinking of Birmingham New Street, mention should be made of the Great Western stations at Snow Hill and Moor Street in Birmingham. Snow Hill seemed to be a cleaner, more open place than New Street and everything about it was so different.

One major difference was the frequency of freight services passing through Snow Hill. Richard Thorne recorded a rare sight of a former LMS 2-6-0 5F 42982 coming through on a coal train.

An earlier picture in September, 1955 the same location briefly caught by Railway Mission Calendar photographer J.D. Gomersall of 2-6-2T No. 6166 shunting a "blood and custard" restaurant car at Snow Hill.

It was a memorable experience for me in the spring of 1987 to walk through the Snow Hill tunnel, and seeing it being

Classes 2p and 3p on the LNWR side (*John Hicks*)

This picture of a Stanier Class "5", mixed traffic engine with Caprotti fitted valve gear is shown on south west relief express service. The Class 5's, many based at Aston, Bescot, and Saltley, were regular sources of power for this holiday type train. In general, West Midland footplate crews found with a few exceptions that the 5's were reliable, flexible, workhorses able to adapt to long distant freight, parcels and semi-fast express services. Something of the period is reflected with gas lighting and a side view of a New Street signal box. It was near this location on the station that I spent quiet evenings in the left luggage department, waiting for the next customer. Back in the late 1950's it seemed railway passengers travelled with far more luggage than they do in the 1990's. I recall some most fascinating pieces of luggage left for months on end until the fines exceeded the value of the suitcases and various packages.

A Caprotti fitted valve gear "Black" waiting to leave with a South West train below a New Street box and amongst gas lights (*John Bassett*)

42982 through Snow Hill (*Richard Thorne*)

A restaurant car being marshalled at Snow Hill *(J.D. Gomersall)*

Mere Hall resting between duties at Snow Hill *(Richard Thorne)*

Midland Pullman service at Snow Hill whilst New Street electrification was in progress *(Richard Thorne)*

5163 about to use one of the two locomotive traversers at Moor Street *(Mike Mensing)*

prepared for the re-opening on October 5th, 1987. BR resident Engineer Tony Cook showed me places where 6″ of soot had to be removed from the roof, dating back to steam days. There was the point where the bullion trains left the main line for the Bank of England's security branch, and Tony showed me the rubber pads under the former Woodside tunnel sleepers to reduce the noise level to those living above the new lines.

Councillor Peter Lister, OBE, in the colourful Midline brochure speaks of Birmingham Snow Hill as "offering, under its "Midline" banner, better service to both the commuter and the shopper heading for the heart of the city, it also displays the potential to develop a further cross-city line".

Further out of the station on the north side our next GWR picture catches 7915 Mere Hall in a break between duties.

An interesting alternative to the King and Castle powered Birmingham-Paddingtons came with the improved WR service into London whilst the Midland Region's electrification scheme was progressing. The faster substitute came in the form of the Midland Pullman shown on an up express service to the Great Western capital.

Moor Street

Birmingham is still reminded of the GWR by the former Moor Street station. I found a different atmosphere there. A former interesting method of allowing an engine to run round its train is seen in the October 1958 view of 2-6-2T 5163, about to use one of the two Moor Street locomotive traverses, taken out in December, 1967.

The opening of Snow Hill and the modern Moor Street again proves that if the public have a regular, reliable, fairly priced rail service they will use it in growing numbers. During my chaplaincy visits to both new stations on the GWR routes, some staff wonder where all their customers are coming from, but welcome them just the same.

There are many other tales to relate about visits in the 1950s and 1980s to Moor Street and Snow Hill but we shall go back to the Royal Town, in those 1950s days.

One of the reasons for writing this book was to record a number of significant events that happened in the 1950s such as (a) the 1953 Coronation; (b) the train disaster in January, 1955; (c) the DMU introduction in March, 1956, and (d) the gathering of scouts from all over the world to celebrate 50 years of scouting at the centenary of their leader Lord Robert Baden-Powell, in August, 1957.

The 1759 New Street to Burton-on-Trent train hauled by 40526 is shown at Sutton Coldfield on 27.7.55 *(John Edgington)*

Chapter Eight

Railway dimensions of the Jamboree

The *Sutton Park — a history and guide* 1966 reprint at 3/6 (17½p) published by the Friends of the Park Association and the Sutton Coldfield News recorded: "the decision to hold this gigantic assembly, which was to be a combination of a Boy Scout Jamboree, a scouters Indaba and a Rover Scout Moot (code name J.I.M.) was only taken in 1955 after sites all over the Midlands had been inspected and evaluated".

Sutton Coldfield, Sutton Park and Streetly Railway Stations were conveniently placed for different entrances into the park. Train services initially brought thousands of scouts from all over the world at the start of the celebrations, took them through the Midlands on excursions, brought in thousands of day visitors from many parts of the contry, and then took thousands of scouters with luggage away again at the end.

At the invitation of Mr. Graham Coombe, the Scout Association's Archivist, I was given access to their records on J.I.M. in London, coming away with the following details. I am indebted to Mr. Coombe for his interest and support. He said he "and thousands of other scouters had very fond memories of the lovely natural Sutton Park".

THE SCOUTER October, 1957

The Indaba — Michael Holmes

". . . on most days, there were excursions arranged and Stratford on Avon, Birmingham, Coventry, London and other parts were visited. Factories and industries in the district readily undertook to open their works to parties of scouts and many took the opportunity thus given them".

Rovermoot — Robin H. Bligh

". . . visits to industry were many and varied, ranging from gasworks and electricity power stations, railway carriage and locomotive works, to factories making typewriters and cardboard boxes".

Scouting Committees

Two of the seven scouting committees for J.I.M. were railway related:
Excursions: J.R.M. Ramshaw as Chairman and C. Nield as Secretary, and
Transport with C.E. Jordan as the Chairman and L. Patrick Secretary.
Industrial pavilion: The industrial pavilion in the Park, included:
Locomotive building: "This stand included models, several of them showing various types of steam, diesel and electric locomotives, produced in Great Britain and used in all parts of the world".
Transport: A demonstration by the British Transport commission showing the services provided by trade and industry, by railways, by road services, docks and inland waterways.
Scout Card System: One card stated that the Chief Scout named a locomotive "Lord Rowallan" at Euston Station on July 16th, 1957.

The Scout's own newspaper, edited by Rex Hazlewood, the Jubilee Journal had a daily circulation of 30,000. It has 24 pages 18″ × 12½″. It recorded "from July 29th the scouts came in trains arriving every 12 minutes, 1,390 came by airlift.

Tuesday, August 6th was Wolf Cub day: 30,000 cubs transformed the normal life of the camp in a way that almost begs a description. No less than 23 special trains were put on by British Railways to cope with the situation; 10,000 came into the camp by special coaches and more came by other means".

Picture log of the Jubilee

"The co-operation of British Railways in this organisation cannot be praised too highly. In every connection they went out of their way to afford us assistance. At the same time it was gratifying to know that they were most impressed by the efficiency of the Scout personnel who handled the arrivals and departures of contingents in Sutton Coldfield".

"In addition to the many local passenger train services which were used for the tranport of individual participants, over 170 special trains were run in connection with J.I.M."

Amended Timetables

The BR Leaflet D.216 printed by Staffordds, of Netherfield, gave special train services and special Cheap Day Fares which applied August 1st-12th, 1957. Most of the day, the normal half hour interval New Street–Sutton Coldfield line service operated. However the Sutton Park line had a much improved service with the last through train to Walsall and

Hampshire scouts on their way to the Jamboree for a day visit. The train began at Portsmouth Harbour *(Ted Higgs)*

Wolverhampton High Level running three hours later than normal.

The special second class cheap day fares between New Street and Penns was 1/4, Sutton Coldfield/Sutton Park 1/6 and to Streetly, Aldridge and Walsall 1/11.

Excursion Examples

The following are examples of three Jubilee Jamboree excursions for those on site:

M.428 Thursday, August 8th
Sutton Park to Bournville, presumably to Cadbury's. The train took 31 minutes.

M.411 Friday, August 9th
Streetly Station to Crewe, believed to have been a visit to the railway works. Journey time 1 hour 24 minutes.

M.803 Friday, August 9th
A 38 minute trip from Sutton Coldfield to Coventry for a visit presumably to the Cathedral/car works.

Each of the excursion tickets enabled the holders to "return by ordinary train without payment", if they missed the designated train. However, they were warned "but only in emergency".

A further excursion photo by Ted records LNER B1 61205 bringing scouts from Cambridge to Sutton.

My brother-in-law, Michael Smith, remembers as a train spotter at the time seeing Royal Scot Class 6P 46169 "The Boy Scout" on a Jamboree special. The Scout HQ confirmed it and that sister engine 46168 "The Girl Guide" was also used.

News Advertisements

The Sutton Coldfield News of Friday, 9th August helps to paint in some background details of the time through its advertisements.

BR ran a diesel train trip from Sutton Coldfield to Alton Towers that weekend for 6/- (30p) return, and a buffet car train from Sutton Coldfield to London at 17/- return, starting from Four Oaks at 9.33 a.m.

A.T. Hastilow's, whose buildings were remarked upon as seen from one of the signal photos, offered their Tudor Rose coach excursions to Leamington Lights for 4/-, Weston-super-Mare 14/-, and Barmouth 14/-, while the Midland Red invited

B1 61205 Jamboree special from Cambridge (*Ted Higgs*)

patronage to the Wye Valley at 30/- (£1.50) including meals, and Colwyn Bay for 14/-.

Any Scouts/leaders wanting a change from J.I.M. could have seen the following films: "Gone with the Wind" (A) at the Sutton Odeon, "The Tommy Steele Story" (U) at the Empress, ABC on the present Sainsbury site, and "The Night the World Exploded" (U) with Kathryn Grant and William Leslie at the Pavilion, Wylde Green.

Scouts and parents who considered returning to Sutton Coldfield to live near the park may have noted these 1957 house prices:

(a) "Well built modern detached 4 bedroom house near the parade — £3,750".

(b) "A Maney Hill Road detached home, 4 bedrooms, 2 reception, bathroom, 2 toilets, built in garage, etc. — £3,750".

(c) "Exceptionally well built detached residence just off Lichfield Road in Jordan Road and close to Four Oaks station — £3,100. 4 bedrooms, 2 secondary bedrooms, etc."

(d) "Freehold dwelling-house near Sutton Coldfield station, excellent condition, 2 living rooms, kitchen, 2 bedrooms, bathroom with w.c. — £1,500".

(e) "3, Royal Road (near the Sutton Park line). Well built large type semi-detached, convenient parade, 3 bedrooms, bathroom 2 reception, breakfast room, kitchen — £1,850".
or a
(f) "Bungalow. Plantsbrook Road, Walmley, superlative modern accommodation. Real bargain £2,680".

Folk were being tempted away from public transport with an advertisement by Wylde Green Engineering Co. Ltd. to buy a Hillman Minx de Luxe at £529 plus £265.17.0 purchase tax totalling £794.17.0, or a new Humber Hawk at £840 plus £421.7.0 purchase tax for a total of £1,261.7.0.

Streetley, Sutton Park, Penns

To keep the trains moving on the Sutton Park line during the intensive J.I.M. services, temporary block posts were set up at Streetly and Penns. Mike Mensing's photograph shows a New Street – Sutton Park – Walsall – Wolverhampton train in the form of a push and pull service propelled by 2-6-2T 41220 on Sunday, August 4th, 1957, at the temporary Streetly block post and ground frame.

Designated Jamboree Stations

Some of the BR background planning is given by Penns Station Master Mr. Les Hollins who took over there just three months before the Jamboree.

"We had District operating Superintendent meetings at which Sutton Park and Streetly were designated Jamboree stations. Both places had a Station Master for the Jamboree with Streetly which was usually covered from Sutton Park, having a relief Station Master in charge.

"The block post at Penns was a former asbestos lamp cabin which was used in the cleaning of signal lamps. In the cabin were two levers and block instruments. The cabin was staffed for 3-4 weeks by two relief Signalmen on 2 × 12 hour shifts.

"At times we had a frequency at Penns of every four minutes. There were some amusing incidents when Jamboree trains were held at Penns whils the previous train was unloaded and cleared from Sutton Park. Some passengers on the specials to Sutton Park thought Penns was Sutton Park Station, because the train stopped there. Scouts and visitors got out and wandered about Penns Station. It took us some time to get them back in. Many of the passengers could not speak English so that complicated communications. The passengers alighted on the left hand side platform, facing Sutton Park in Mr. Hollins photograph of Penns Station.

My shot in 1983, gives a modern contrast of the same location.

As Penns appeared to have little public documented history about it, I shall return to share further information on that Midland Railway built station from Les Hollins' extensive recollections.

The Scouts' undiscovered resource

A most fascinating fact about the J.I.M. was shared with me by Ken Beasley. On two occasions during the days just before the Jamboree was officially opened, he relieved as driver with fireman Hocking on two Jamboree passenger specials around 6.30 p.m. at Aston No. 1 signalbox, the one that operated movements to Aston MPD and the Stechford line.

The foreign engines came from the London area on London Dock Specials.

"After a 2-3 minute briefing by the departing crew from the Eastern/Southern loco, we took the train from the Junction, past No. 1 and No. 2 boxes and onto Bescot, Walsall, then through Streetly to the Jamboree unloading point on the up line, about 1½ miles from Sutton Park Station.

"The unloading point never appeared in the public timetables and many railway staff working in the area was not aware of its existence. The unloading point was built of sleepers, not unlike Butlers Lane which was put up one weekend as a temporary measure". Arthur Spencer provides us with a record of Butlers Lane being built in 1956.

Driver Beasley told me "Staff were taken with the many coloured folk, because there were not many around in 1957. The overseas scouts had their tea chests, kit bags, etc.,

unloaded at the isolated unloading platform. Because of the length of the train, it had to pull up at least twice.

"As a former Midland driver I knew the Birmingham-Derby main line, so was able to take the ECS onto Burton-on-Trent for disposal".

The information from Mr. Beasley was a complete surprise because there was no mention of the platform in the Scouts

Some Jamboree visitors mistook Penns for Sutton Park Station *(Les Hollins)*

New Street to Wolverhampton Jamboree push and pull service, showing temporary block post at Streetly *(Mike Mensing)*

Penns Station site in 1983 *(John Bassett)*

HQ records. Sutton Park signalman at the time Charles Curtis had no recollections, neither did Penn's Station Master Les Hollins. Mr. Ernie Hankin at Sutton Park remembered that the platform had been proposed but turned down by district management.

Presuming I had overlooked the item, I wrote to Graham Coombe, who responded "the remarks made recently by a former Railway engine driver are fascinating for we have been unable to find any reference to an off loading point for heavy equipment between Streetly and Sutton Park Stations in any of the official reports that were compiled after J.I.M. and had there been I feel sure it would have been recorded".

Graham in his usual helpful custom approached the person who would know. In this case Mr. Ken Stevens, the Organising Commissioner of J.I.M. who was presented to the Queen during Her Majesty's visit to the Park. The Sutton Coldfield News quoted the OC as "the busiest man of the lot" — at J.I.M.

Official scout opinion about the phantom platform

Mr. Stevens replied "I think Mr. Bassett in his question about a Railway off loading point is confused. What British Rail did was to build a footpath from Streetly Station under the nearby railway bridge up into Sutton Park. This was primarily to enable us to use that station for despatching campers on day railway trips without them having to cross a busy main road.

"It may have been true that this footpath was used by the Railway for off loading heavy equipment, but I do not remember any such thing taking place. For one thing, our baggage centre was right at the other end of the camp — almost two miles away, and it would have been simpler and presumably less costly, to have off-loaded heavy baggage at Sutton Park Station".

Having read the relevant letter sections to Mr. Beasley he still remained adamant that the off loading point was a separate location from the one Mr. Stevens referred to. The Assistant Train Crew Manager at Birmingham, Mr. Harry Pratt recalled the off loading point and the flagmen who were placed there to signal the trains.

The former Sutton Coldfield PW man, Walter Roberts advised me that he was one of the flagmen at the platform. The flagman remembered that at one time the sleepers had a tarpaulin over them for protection and security.

It does seem strange that BR and the Scouts Association had not liaised over such an important location.

The approximate location of the off loading platform is seen in this picture by Richard Thorne of a LCGB special

approaching Streetly hauled by 44944. The possible site is not too difficult to find because it was near an underbridge with open parkland either side, between Sutton Park and Streetly Stations.

Retired engine driver from Saltley, Bill Alcock informed me, "I recall the Boy Scouts' Jamboree where special trains were run from different Ports throughout the country. Train crews from depots such as Stoke-on-Trent, Gloucester, etc. who did not normally work over the line were sent to learn the route of the line prior to the Jamboree. A special platform was built about 1 mile from Streetly station near to the farmer's crossing, and gates for both sides of the park. I can recall working a train at the end of the Jamboree. We collected the carriages and luggage vans from Saltley carriage sidings, picking up at the special platform. I think the train was going to Liverpool docks. We went via Aldridge, Pleck Junction, to Portobello Junction avoiding Wolverhampton and on to Crewe".

The late John Ford of the LMR HQ at Quayside Tower, Birmingham, loaned me a number of important 1950's documents. The following quote is from his copy of Trains Illustrated Vol X, No. 109 of October, 1957, Pages 560-61 published by Ian Allen Ltd.

Train Spotters Observations

"The Scout Jamboree at Sutton Coldfield resulted in an extensive programme of special workings. The normal Birmingham (New Street)-Walsall service via Sutton Park of some eight trains a day each way was suspended and replaced by an interval auto-train service, and Bescot area shed allocations were temporarily augmented, the Walsall additions including Class "2" 2-6-2 tanks Nos. 41212/20/24 and 41320 and Class "2" 2-6-0 No. 78055. An industrious correspondent recorded the arrival and departure of no fewer than 187 specials at Streetly and Sutton Park between July 29th and August 14th, and more ran unrecorded after dark; origins and destinations covered the whole country, and sheds represented by the motive power ranged from Bath and Birkenhead to Carnforth and Carlisle.

"An outstanding event on August 1st was the through working of a V.I.P. train from St. Pancras to Sutton Park by the newly named "Britannia", No. 70045, and its return from Streetley that evening. Amongs the other visitors on August 4th a C.L.C. engine arrived, No. 45333 (8E) on a special from Baguley, on August 6th came a Southport train with a Southport engine, No. 45061, on August 7th Jubilee No. 45600 (10C) worked throughout from Millom in Cumberland (now Cumbria) to Streetley and back; and on August 13th "Royal Scot" No. 46135 (5A) took out a special for Newcastle

Butlers Lane under construction *(Arthur Spencer)*

via Derby, Nos. 46111/64/8 were also recorded on the Aston-Lichfield line during the Jamboree, the last of them on a Girl Guides' special from Windsor; in all three cases the stock was taken on from Sutton Coldfield empty to Burton, the engines being serviced at Burton shed, where Pacific No. 70045 was noted after working an excursion from Willesden to Sutton Coldfield on August 4th. A "B1" No. 61205 also travelled the Aston-Lichfield line".

The main alternative enthusiast's periodical The Railway Magazine reported in September, 1957 issue under London Midland Region notes, p. 665, "At a ceremony at Euston station on July 16th, Lord Rowallan, Chief Scout, gave his name to Britannia Class 4-6-2 locomotive No. 70045, which entered service on the London Midland Region in June, 1954. A 'guest locomotive' present was 'Royal Scot' Class 4-6-0 No. 46169 The Boy Scout, the nameplate plaques on which had been unveiled at Euston by the former Chief Scout in December, 1930. Lord Rowallan was used to haul special trains to the Boy Scout International Jubilee Jamboree at Sutton Park in August".

Bill Alcock, his wife and two children visited the Jamboree. "We entered the park at the Streetley entrance and walked through the whole encampment. We talked to scouts from many different countries. It took us about four hours before we emerged at the Sutton Town entrance. That night a thunderstorm flooded the park".

During the Jamboree, very shortly before I left the railway I did some ticket inspection duties at Sutton Park. I had a chance to experience the special occasion, meeting folk from a variety of locations in the United Kingdom and abroad. The tickets I handled came from a wide selection of places. It was an enjoyable experience.

The Park station was noisy at times with the scouts and visitors, though it could, like Four Oaks a few years before it, soon return to a quiet wayside rural scene. I think it was at Sutton Park that I noticed one of the American scouts discarding a sausage roll as a food item he did not like in his packed meal. Apparently a considerable amount of food was wasted by overseas visitors who could not adapt to some of our food.

Retired Signalman Curtis told me the Jamboree "trains kept going, one after another. But it took some trains up to 10 false starts to get away, because scouts kept running onto the platforms to get on".

Jamboree Dispersal

The dispersal operators on August 13th/14th gave the scouts a coloured card to denote their departure station, such as:

Red — Sutton Coldfield
Yellow — Streetly
Blue — Sutton Park

The scouts were advised to arrive at the two Sutton stations one hour before departure and Streetly, 40 minutes.

Tom Samsom's photograph gives a view of the one hour wait at the Station Street entrance to Sutton Coldfield Station. The building is still about the same but the access is now blocked off and looks unsightly.

The nearness of the administrative centre of the Town Hall can be gained by the turret seen above the station entrance. This is the same entrance that was locked up when the Sutton Coldfield police officers ran the 50 yards from the police station to the railway station on Sunday, 23rd January, 1955.

44944 near disputed offloading luggage platforms between Sutton Park and Streetly *(Richard Thorne)*

Red card holders wait for their return Jamboree services from Sutton Coldfield *(T. Samsom)*

It was stated in the News in 1958 that the Scout Organisation was disappointed that the expected 100,000 visitors to the Jamboree did not materialise. 81,000 visited. Learning from Sutton's Jamboree, the scouts decided future such events "would be on a much smaller scale".

Looking back 30 years later, the Jamboree was a massive undertaking by British Railways, but again it reflected the major place the railway industry held in transport in the late 1950's.

Arthur Spencer's photograph at Sutton Park Station brings the focus on the J.I.M. to a conclusion. This shot shows 4-6-0 "Jubilee" Class 45598 "Basutoland" arriving with M.406 for some of the waiting scouts, whilst others, presumably for later services, walk across the footbridge.

Similar to Penns for Walmley, there does not seem to be much information gathered in an easily accessible form on Sutton Park, so we will reconsider that station in more depth later.

Jubilee 45598 "Basutoland" arriving at Sutton Park with yet another Jamboree special *(Arthur Spencer)*

Chapter Nine

Railway activities for Sutton youngsters

My railway career in August, 1957, as a relief travelling ticket collector was coming to an end, at my choosing. In my leisure time, I worshipped at Duke Street Chapel, in Sutton Coldfield, helped as a Sunday School teacher and was a member of a national boys' club organisation called The Covenanters. One games evening in 1956, Baptist lay preacher John Edwards, who regularly preached at the earlier Duke Street Hall, then the later Duke Street Chapel, brought along his younger son to join the group.

The Covenanter leaders were pleased to see the lad for that session, but regretted he could not come again because he was too young. I felt God was speaking to me that night as a committed Christian, to start a club for boys 10-13 years old at Duke Street Chapel. One of the major reasons that prevented me from working with others to open such a club was the railway shifts I worked.

After 18 months an opportunity arose for me in September, 1957, to work as a warehouseman with the Halford Cycle

"Midland Red" garage visit (*John Bassett*)

Company. With three other young men, a lot of leaning on God and a supportive Church fellowship, the club for Junior Covenanters opened, and my enjoyable rail career stopped.

It was a mystery to me for many years why I went on the railway, giving up a promising career seven years later, just to help with a boys' club. But time often shows God's reasoning. A plan begins to emerge as we trust Him. A simple but true chorus we used to sing in the Boy Covenanter Group has helped me so many times. "Trust and obey, for there's no other way to be happy in Jesus, than to trust and obey".

Looking back more than 30 years later, as a Railway Chaplain, it is now clear God has used my railway background, and subsequent practice and training in social work, adult education and training in management to equip me in a unique way for this ministry he called me to. During the course of his leading I have gained insight and experience of railway employment from the bottom to the top.

Railway staff and enthusiasts ask me how do I get my guidance from God. Surely that is old fashioned! To many it is. Two verses assist me and I go back to them time and again for refreshed help. "Trust in the Lord with all your heart and lean not on your own understanding; in all your ways acknowledge Him, and he will make your paths straight". Proverbs 3 : 5-6.

This group are seen at Exmouth Junction M.P.D. (*John Bassett*)

Junior Covenanter Activities

In the next four years 1957-61 before I took up my first full time professional social work position, the Junior Covenanter group progressed. Fortunately for me, many of the lads were rail enthusiasts, so half day, full day, a weekend and a week's holiday were involved with railway activities.

The following photographs indicate some of the locations and Sutton Coldfield lads who went on the visits.

The boys and some of the leaders enjoyed the assortment of visits to a variety of railway installations on the group's holiday. Staying with the Southern Region these 13 Jucos, perhaps rather dangerously, stand in front of 92112, near the coaling plant at Exmouth Junction shed.

Assisting at one of the holidays was my wife-to-be Joan (left) and my cousin Ann, seen with seven Jucos awaiting a train at Exeter, St. David's making the most of an empty GWR barrow (*John Bassett*)

Jucos visit to an I.O.W. depot (*John Bassett*)

The railway holidays were a time of considerable excitement for the boys, and a cause of much jealously amongst their train-spotting mates who did not belong to the Duke Street Chapel Juco group. The membership came from a number of areas in Sutton, and included lads like myself from working class homes, mixing with fellows from fairly well off to very well off families. It was noticeable that amongst the four leaders any boy was able to identify with at least one of the young staff. As a staff team we needed on occasions to pray particularly hard to work as a team for the benefit of all the lads. A number of boys interested in the wide variety of pursuits we offered were put off by the christian dimension of the club. However, many found the balanced programme quite tolerable and a number received help in their formative years from the christian teaching. Happily, the Juco group at Duke Street Chapel continues in the 1990's.

This next picture goes back to a Juco week-end in North Wales. The group of three including my brother-in-law to be Michael Smith in the centre are taking numbers at the main MPD in the area, Llandudno Junction (7A) which had rows of locos to note.

Some of the Jucos in the 1950's and early 1960's were interested in many forms of transport and one print shows four of the lads at the time visiting a Warwickshire "Midland Red" garage with one of the company's own built coaches.

A feature of the Junior Covenanters is the width of interests served including sports. They have a fast and furious indoor game called Juknockey which is sometimes played at the area rallies. Our Sutton group had some good wins and painful losses.

Between 1957-61 I travelled daily to Birmingham by the DMU service, keeping up to date with what was happening and frequently visiting Sutton Park station, which is now covered in more depth.

Three spotters at Llandudno Junction (*John Bassett*)

Chapter Ten

Sutton Town, the forgotten station

Mr. Rex Christiansen provides the background picture for us in the already mentioned "The West Midlands".

"The London and North Western Railway bought the Wolverhampton and Walsall Railway in 1875, and sold it a year later to the Midland Railway, which had reached Walsall from the opposite direction with a line from Castle Bromwich, built by the Wolverhampton, Walsall and Midland Junction, authorised on August 6th, 1872. Although the company was nominally independent it had strong ties with the Midland and an agreement of December 1872 led to the small company's absorption two years later".

The line's promoters received a hostile reception from the public when it was realised that the route ran through part of the beloved Sutton Park. However, the objections were withdrawn when cheaper coal was to be one of the advantages of having that traffic go by rail.

The Midland bought a strip of land in the park almost two miles in length for £6,500 and the result, claimed a local historian, was a "horrible scar on the face of Sutton Park, only softened by the passage of time during the growth of many fine trees along its course". Speaking of the route through the park since the withdrawal of the passenger service in 1965, Hilda M.

A bird's-eye view of the healed terrible scar! *(Thomson Directories)*

58

Moss wrote "we can see how that once-detested construction has been absorbed by nature, to add another touch to the varied beauty of our park".

The route softened by the passage of time is visible in the birds eye view kindly donated by Thomson Directories. The railway is seen coming in from the top left hand corner in a straight line, taking it past Blackroot Pool, the parcels distribution centre at Sutton Park Station, and leaving the scene in the middle of the right hand side by the former Town Station in Midland Drive.

"The Midland" continues Mr. Christiansen on Page 109 "opened the WW&M from Castle Bromwich to Walsall on July 1st, 1879. Five intermediate stations — Penns, Sutton Coldfield, Sutton Park, Streetly and Aldridge — were served by trains between New Street and Wolverhampton High Level. They reversed in and out of Walsall, though through running, avoiding the station, was possible over a stretch opened at the same time between Lichfield Road and North Walsall Junctions. From January 1st, 1990 Midland trains were switched to the LNWR route between Walsall and Wolverhampton, and some LNWR services began using the Midland via Willenhall to avoid reversal".

Mr. Geoff Hughes, retired from the LMR HQ Public Affairs Department at Stanier House, Birmingham, advised me some while ago that "the Sutton Coldfield station was of course Midland Railway and renamed Sutton Town on June 2nd, 1924". Which incidentally was only seven months before it closed!

Sutton Town Station — Public Opinion Changes

A number of accounts of the opening of the Sutton Park line includes the general public's initial hostility, but none I have read recall a complete turn around 46 years later and nothing when the Town station was reopened a further 30 years later in 1955 as stated by Bill Alcock.

The example is given in the minutes of a Sutton Coldfield Town Council meeting held on Wednesday, December 3rd, 1924, in the Town Hall. The Town Clerk presented a petition of nine forms signed by 566 persons.

The petition read "The Major and Members of the Borough Council of Sutton Coldfield, we the undersigned, being residents of the Borough of Sutton Coldfield, have heard, with regret, that it is proposed to close the Town (Midland) Station as from the 1st January next, and strongly urge the Borough Council to take every possible step to prevent such a course being taken. Your petitioners state that they are in the habit of using such station, and they would experience much difficulty and hardship should the same be closed.

The Major moved "That the Council have received the extensively signed petition against closing of the Town Midland Station, do hereby strongly oppose the closing, and urge the Railway Company to reconsider their decision, and that the Town Clerk be instructed to send a copy of it to the Company. Alderman Vale seconded".

Sutton Town Closure

The station was closed by the LMS on January 1st, 1925. It may be that the directors of the 1923 formed LMS had identified stations and services, such as Sutton Coldfield (LNWR) and Sutton Coldfield (later Town) (MR) which provided duplicate services for New Street Station, and rather than make an unnecessary loss closed at least one station.

My thanks to Robert Paddison a professional railway manager with responsibilities for the Sutton Park line who has kindly donated a number of prints from slides. It must be stressed that these photographs were taken as part of Mr. Paddison's employment on BR property, and are not in any way to be taken by readers as an invitation to trespass on rail property to gain such photographic records.

A January, 1983, photograph shows the front downside building in Midland Drive, which had been used for the employment exchange, offices and a hairdressers.

Mr. Paddison's rear view of the downside buildings helps us realise that the former Town station is at least in as good a state of repair than remaining buildings at Sutton Coldfield (LNWR), Four Oaks and Sutton Park.

Railside view of Sutton Town downside building (*Robert Paddison*)

Midland Drive entrance (*John Bassett*)

Upside Frontage (*Robert Paddison*)

Conservation Involvement

In the 1970's conservationists Tony and Mary Cadwallader and another couple in South Drive, Sutton Coldfield, bought a plot of land including the upside buildings of the former Town station of just under three acres, so as to conserve and protect that area from development. Tony advised me that 35 species of trees including the tree of heaven had been identified in the plot. There was some wild garlic and a huge area of bluebells. Mrs. Cadwallader speaking of the wild life around remembers "one lunchtime a fox coming to the house, which backed onto the railway line".

The next photo shows the front entrance into the upside Town station on a winter's day.

The upside (to Birmingham) building was frequently vandalised by children and "once they tried to set the station on fire". Mr. Cadwallader also noticed "that the gent's toilets were not served by mains water. Rain water was collected into a tank then flushed as required".

The previous owner of the site, Mr. Gerald Cattell had many railway relics in the upside station building. Former Sutton Park signalman Charlie Curtis could recall "plans by Mr. Cattell to have a preserved steam locomotive on display at the upside building". The large collection of relics was sold

after his death in 1977. One wonders if any of those relics reached an American restaurant which has a Sutton Coldfield nameboard amongst other items which my father-in-law Cyril Smith has seen.

Part of the deteriorating condition of the upside Town station (*Robert Paddison*)

Chapter Eleven

Sutton Park station in war and peace

We now return the ¾ mile on the downline to the site of the former Sutton Park station. In the 1950's and still in the 1990's one can approach it from a path leading off Anchorage Road to the right of the Station Master's house. The 1987 shot still picks out the route down the tree lined path to the station below.

Mike Mensing includes the station end of the path in his fine photograph of tender first 0-8-0 48964 "trundling through Sutton Park station with a westbound freight on May 30th, 1959".

A distant view of the path under the footbridge is seen in John Edgington's photo of 42604 from Walsall (3C) shed in Platform 3.

These 1935 LMS introduced 2-6-4T, 4p locos could be warm in the winter, but very stifling for the footplate crew in the hot weather. On this occasion, probably a Sunday, the train will be going to Walsall and Wolverhampton high level.

Parcels Depot

In the 1950's, Sutton Park station was known in the town as a parcel depot. Mr. S. Evans, Assistant Head Postmaster at the Head Post Office, Birmingham, shares information available on the parcels depot:

"As far as it is known locally the site was originally used as a coal depot. Although one of the buildings on the site is some

90-100 years old, the majority of the buildings were built in the early 1940's to house a Forces Post Office, German prisoners-of-war being used to assist in the construction. There has been some additional building since then. The US Army (Postal Force) took over the buildings in 1942/3 to deal with correspondence and parcels belonging to forces personnel missing or killed in action during the war. Local civilians were employed to assist together with members of the Birmingham Road Post Office staff.

Looking down from Anchorage Road *(John Bassett)*

A freight trundling through Sutton Park *(Mike Mensing)*

Sutton Park station *(John Edgington)*

"The Post Office building was used from early 1947 to early 1948 for the British Army Post Office and then reverted to Post Office use in 1948 to deal with British Commonwealth, Foreign and Forces parcels. Since 1954 the depot had been used as a foreign postal office of exchange for incoming and outgoing letters and parcels.

"The depot receives parcels for distribution in the United Kingdom from various countries including much of the "old commonwealth", USA, Sweden and Norway. Parcels are despatched to a number of "old commonwealth" countries and letters to various countries including China, Japan, North and East Africa and the Middle East. Currently about 5,000 parcels are received from abroad weekly rising to some 25,000 a week, prior to Christmas. Current levels of postings (August 1983) for abroad are approximately 250 bags of parcels and 2,000 bags of letter mail weekly. I am sorry we do not have such figures for the 1950's and 1960's. The depot has approximately 100 staff including Customs Officers who subject parcels to examination before clearance. The depot is now used exclusively to serve the postal depot".

Mr. Evans I understand has moved to Gloucester, but the manager of the Sutton Park site, Mr. F.E. Heath advised me in 1990 of a number of changes.

"The daily parcels train finished about three years ago and everything now is roaded from this depot". The items of mail had increased significantly in the last seven years but since "December 29th, 1989, the customs presence had ceased and the Sutton Park depot is known as the 'Birmingham Office of Exchange for Surface Mail' which is world wide", so with the closing of the parcel examination service at Sutton Park another important connection with the past has finished.

The close working between BR staff and the Post Office demonstrated in the photograph of Sutton Park signalma, Charlie Curtis receiving his 40 years Service Award from th Area Manager, surrounded by PO staff from the Sutton Par depot.

Sutton Park in the war

Mrs. Joan Price of Jerome Road was one of three wome covering the 3 × 8 hour shifts in Sutton Park signal box i WWII. Her colleagues being Louise Hall and Eileen Kirkhar Joan told me that "some older railwaymen discriminate against the women for taking signalling positions. Th administration staff from Curzon Street and Lawley Stree goods depots were transferred to Sutton Park station buildin after they had been bombed out to carry out the same work i offices on the down and up sides at Sutton Park.

"If a 'red alert' bombing raid warning in the night wa received from Saltley the signal person rang the platform be to wake up the fire watchers from the goods department".

The shot of Stanier 2-6-4T, No. 42482 on the 2.01 t· Birmingham by Mr. Russell includes some of the goods admi office accommodation on the upside and Midland box in whic Mrs. Price worked.

Troop trains were regular users of the Midland route in th war. The "signal staff" continued Mrs. Price "had to give the priority and carefully listened for the engine whistle code indicating which route they needed: Camp Hill or New Street

"Sometimes on nights she could hear the rats playing aroun the signal chairs underneath the box". On other occasion

hen it was moonlight Joan saw "the rats playing on and
ound the railway lines".

"In the war years," she told me "there were not many fitters
out so the engines were in bad condition, with as much
eight put behind them as the officers thought could be
lled".

oyal train

the 1940's Charlie Curtis remembers that "King George VI
d the present Queen, the Queen's Mother, were in the royal
ain for an overnight stop in the Sutton Park siding.
nfortunately as the light engine placed there in advance to
pply the train with heating, failed, so the train engine had to
ovide the night heating".

According to Mr. Curtis "the special and private notices
out the royal train's overnight stay stated drivers must not
und their whistles that night. However the Wellingborough-
escot freight driver sounded the engine whistle as usual as the
ain approached Sutton Park, and someone complained to the
spector who had fallen asleep in the box at the time. Mr.
urtis heard the whistle. The Inspector being asleep at the time
vised control "he had not heard any whistle". According to
hn Hicks, the previous Sutton Royal stopover occurred
hen King George V in WWI stayed overnight at Richard
ooper's home and the train was stabled at Four Oaks station.

In the 1950's Mr. Hankin the Sutton Park Station Master
called "that there was a daily parcels service" to his station
rriving at 7.35 a.m. and returning to Birmingham at 5.40 p.m.

Guards Training School

After the Admin staff returned to Birmingham, Sutton Park
was used for two further functions. Mr. Curtis, again "There
was a Guards Training School on the upside". The instructors
told the Signalman that "the Indian trainees made the best use
of the training opportunities".

Driving School

Charlie also recalls "The Motor School where the trainees
learnt on three wheel mechanical horses, with Mr. Booth in
charge".

In answer to my request to Mr. Norman Fowler MP for
Sutton Coldfield on the Driving School details, Dr. J.D.C.A
Prideaux of BR wrote "The Driving School at Sutton Park was
set up in the early 1950's for the purpose of training railway
motor vehicle drivers. At that time it was difficult to recruit
men for this work and so new entrants to railway service were
trained up to the required standard on British Rail motor
vehicles of all types. To the best of my knowledge the school
closed in the mid 1960's".

Station Master Hankin gave further details "Number of
vehicles in use 8; number of driving instructors 2; number of
driving trainees at a time 8; length of course 4 weeks;" Mr.
Hankin commented "If the trainee did not show signs of
making a driver after two weeks he was returned to his depot.
But he could apply again after a certain period of time. The

To the left of the signal box was a dining car providing meals for admin staff transferred after being bombed out *(Eric S. Russell)*

School had its own Driver Examiner who had the authority to pass men out as drivers".

Sutton Park/Streetly staffing

Thinking about the station staff, Mr. Hankin had an establishment at Sutton Park for "3 signalpersons and 2 porters". As the Station Master responsible for Streetly there were 2 porteress posts and he told me proudly "Streetly Station won the Shield and prizes for the Best Kept Station, 2 years running". The Sutton Coldfield News of October 7th, 1955 confirmed "that Streetly had won the Best Kept Station Competition award in the Birmingham (Midland) District for the second year in succession. Streetly also won second prize for cleanliness and tidiness".

Passenger Services Timetables

The 1952 and 1960 weekly times are given from Sutton Park:

To Walsall

June–Sept. 1952

a.m.		p.m.		SX	SO		
7.44	8.34	12.45	1.24	1.36	5.55	7.00	

Dec. 1960

a.m.		p.m.		SO		
7.42	8.32	12.43	1.29	6.2	7.6	

To Birmingham

June–Sept. 1952

	SX					SX	SO
6.51	7.8	8.26	2.3		6.8	7.13	7.16

Dec. 1960

	SO				
7.1	8.20	2.2	6.11	7.10	

According to the timetables the 1952 mileage of 18¾ mile had increased to 19 miles in 1960! Journey times showed speeding up over the eight years by five minutes on some runs which probably reflects the introduction of the DMU's.

The 1952 summer service shows a Saturdays only (SO holiday train leaving Walsall at 6.35 a.m., calling all station including Sutton Park at 6.51, reaching New Street at 7.2 a.m. After an eight minutes wait it went on to Kingswear i Devon arriving at 2.05 p.m. The 207¾ miles taking 9½ hours.

Excursions

Thinking about far away places, my mother wrote to BI requesting train excursions from Sutton Park and secured number to places like Weston-super-Mare which we patronised as a family. There were a few most summers and some on the LNWR line.

The weekday passenger service on the Sutton Park line wa mainly used by commuters but reflecting on "Bank holiday and Sundays" Mr. Hankin said "services ran during the summer bringing hundreds of passengers from Wolverhampton and Walsall".

Charlie Curtis presentation *(British Rail)*

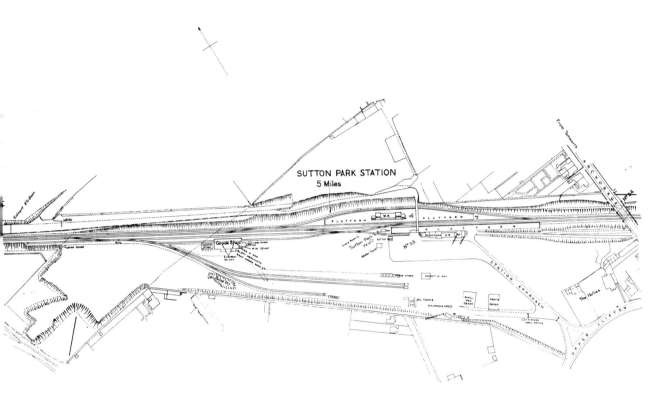

SUTTON PARK STATION
5 Miles

An April 1951 plan of Sutton Coldfield Station *(LMR)*

Freight side

In the 1950's the "promised cheap supply of coal" was still arriving and passing through Sutton Park from the nearby Aldridge Colliery area.

"A 'daily tripper' ran from Water Orton to Aldridge and returned to Washwood Health with coal from Aldridge Colliery" commented Mr. Hankin. It was from that service "coal was supplied to Crees, Davenport and Walsall Co-op. The station was also supplied with freight wagons for W. Crees, the building merchant".

Summer Saturdays

Just as the Sutton Park line was used for vital troop and freight services during WWII, many important Saturday relief trains were regularly routed past Blackroot pool on Summer Saturdays in the 1950's. I spent many an enjoyable Saturday afternoon sitting on a Sutton Park station platform bench seeing the Pines Express and other fast services tearing through as seen in John Hick's action shot of the pines, south westbound. Some parcels vans are in the bay platform.

Signalman Curtis said "on a summer Saturday two light engines went up together towards Walsall then later brought down a portion each of the pines express. They really sped

down the straight line from Streetly. You should have seen the last coach whip round the bend" towards the Town Station.

Sutton Park had a country charm about it, though Mr. Robert Powell Hendry though it was "exceptionally plain for the Midland. Perhaps the most interesting item is the sign in the middle of the recessed portion, which is a BR totem superimposed upon a rectangular board. The totem would bear the station name and this particular combination is somewhat uncommon". Mr. Edgington gives a summer memory of the 5.17 p.m. Wolverhampton to New Street pulled by 42429 at Sutton Park on July 27th, 1955. One of the totems referred to can be seen on the LMS noticeboard above the loco's steam dome. The railway fence separating the path leading from the station into the park can be seen above the variety of train coaches. The LMS had been absorbed into British Railways seven years before, so the noticeboards were on the way to being collectors items!

The type of platform seat at Sutton Park is shown by Mike Mensing in his focus on the Midland Railway company water column on the up platform. The water column was at least 36 years old at the time of the 1959 shot. The braziers as mentioned in details about Four Oaks, were used in very cold weather to prevent the water freezing.

Reg Bevan, one of the Birmingham New Street learning instructor team, just along from my office in the project suite on Platform 1B, remembers firing 41902 of Bescot shed on the Sunday, Walsall-Sutton Park push-pull specials, doing seven return trips. He told me "41902 went like a deer but it was called 'the water cart' because it used a lot of water. We dare not pass a water column en route because it you did, she would run out of water and drop a plug. That would mean a new fire box, becoming an expensive job".

Retired Bill Alcock was working a "freight train via the Sutton Park Line. We were stopped at Sutton Park Signal Box and informed that cattle had been reported on the line before us. On going through the first bridge we saw about six cows in front of us. No matter how slow or how faster we tried to run, the cattle kept on the line in front of us. After a long while we approached the farm crossing, so I said to my fireman if we don't get them into the park they will be in front of us up to Aldridge. So we stopped the train, opened the gate at one side of the park, and attempted to round them up and send them into the park which was longer than anticipated. One Hereford would not go in but fortunately the guard had walked up to see what we were up to. With his help we managed to get the last one in the park". When the train reached the next open box at Ryecroft the signalman told driver Alcock off for taking more than an hour longer booked. When the signalman recognised Bill he said "What have you done with the cattle, cut them up, to take them back to your mates at Saltley!"

Mr. Curtis serviced the twelve lamps and four dummies each week on overtime. He used longlite fuel in the Adlake lamps.

"The Pines" express racing through Sutton Park (*John Hicks*)

42429 at Sutton park (*John Edgington*)

John Hicks, the Sutton Coldfield businessman is seen looking at some railway company coats of arms. He sells railway plaques, railway ties, badges, etc., in his Sutton premises, and donated a number of photos for this book.

The picture includes a number of parcel vans at the goods depot and a "Mickey Mouse" on a Walsall bound train.

The gradual decline of the Sutton Park downside buildings has been evident over many years. However, I was surprised to see the car park almost full one Wednesday in 1989. A PO worker told me that with the additional long vehicles brought in to transport the mail that normally went by rail on that railway strike day, staff cars had to be parked in the station car park so the extra lorries had room. Considering the state of the buildings it is amazing part of them are still used. One wonders if there is a preservation order on the 1879 station?

A railside impression of July 1984 shows the other side of the building, part of it still being used in 1990 by LCP Fuels.

Mr. Paddison's picture on page 69, catches a class 45 just passing the downside buildings, and the top of the incline through the two bridges in the background. The photo also includes the cross over and the staggered platforms. The dining car was parked in the downside bay to feed the reaccommodated bombed out goods staff from Curzon Street and Lawley Street in WWII.

Permanent Way Engineer (North) Robert Paddison's shot of the Sutton Park goods shed gives an inside impression through the conveniently open doors.

An impression of the goods shed in steam days with the sorting office accommodation as well is seen in Richard Thorne's photo in 1965.

Fireman's memories of Sutton Park line

I am grateful to the late John Ford for two further significant items. The first is his written extracts from the diary he kept as a locomotive fireman, earning £6.13.6 a week in Fenruary, 1955 at the age of 17.

John's second item, a diagram of the Sutton Park signal box in May, 1959, could have taken place when Mr. Curtis was on duty.

Bridging the gap between the 1950's and the 1990's at Sutton Park Station we have the Surface Mail Sorting Office of the Post Office and the LCP Fuels ordering office in the 1879 Midland Railway building.

Midland railway water column (*Mike Mensing*)

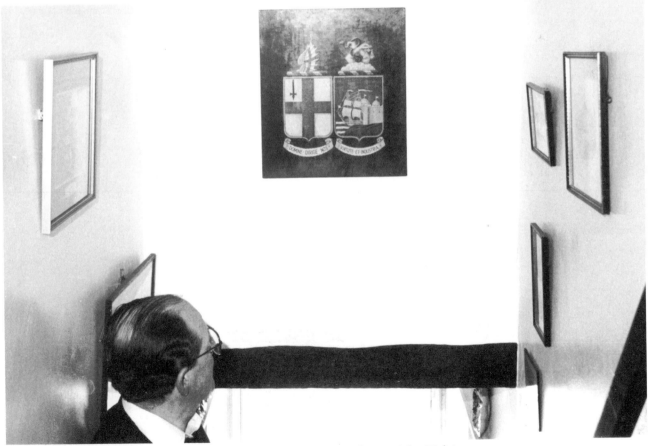

Sutton Coldfield businessman John Hicks looking at Railway coats of arms (*John Hicks*)

"Mickey Mouse" on the Walsall service at Sutton Park (*John Hicks*)

Overgrown view of Sutton Park station from the car park, in 1982 (*John Bassett*)

The remaining Sutton Park building from the railside (*John Bassett*)

The second picture includes the LCP Fuels display in the same room, giving some brightness to an otherwise decaying building.

Mr. Lamb advised me that it is a busy freight line. There appeared to be four trains each hour. I have been there with a variety of locos/stock going past. A class 55 went through one lunch time on its way towards the former Sutton Town station.

This is an interesting view from the 1879 Midland line between Sutton Park and Sutton Town stations, seen by freight train crews of the DMUs on the frequent Cross City link services, using the 1884 extension by the LNWR

A comparison of the Sutton Park and Sutton Town stations shows a number of similarities. Researchers and Model Railway people will also recognise the basic Midland Railway pattern in Arthur Spencer's picture of Streetly in readiness for Jamboree trains. The photo shows the signal cabin at the other end of Platform 2 and "the two signals to help create a block post".

Anyone looking for a concise history of Sutton Coldfield (LNWR) Four Oaks, Sutton Park, Gravelly Hill, Erdington, Chester Road, Wylde Green and Lichfield City stations with drawings/photos could find the Hendry book a wealth of information. However up to now I have only found the occasional published photo about the next Sutton Coldfield suburban station to be considered : Penns for Walmley.

Sutton Park Goods shed *(Robert Paddison)*

Class 45 Diesel passing down bay platform *(Robert Paddison)*

Print *(Richard Thorne)*

Mr. A. Lamb, the manager at the Sutton Park site at his desk *(John Bassett)*

MONDAY 28ᵀᴴ FEBRUARY 1955
 ON DUTY   3/30 P.M.   OFF DUTY 11/30 P.M.
 ENGINE 43046. IVATT CLASS 4 2-6-0. 21A
 LIGHT ENGINE FROM BOURNVILLE SHED TO KINGS NORTON.
 EMPTY COACHES TO NEW ST.   WORK 6/42 ALL STATIONS
 VIA PENNS TO WALSALL.   LEAVE COACHES IN PLATFORM 5 AT
 WALSALL.   LIGHT ENGINE TO SALTLEY VIA PENNS.   DISPOSE.
 SNOW.   DRIVER BERT PREECE 367.
 FIRST TRIP ON A "DOODLEBUG". DIFFICULTY WITH STEAM.
 ALSO FIRST TRIP TO WALSALL.

TUESDAY 1ˢᵀ MARCH 1955
 ON DUTY 3/30 P.M.   OFF DUTY 11/30 P.M.
 ENGINE 42337 FOWLER CLASS 4 2-6-4 TANK. 21A
 GOOD TRIP. LOTS OF STEAM.   DRIVER BERT PREECE 367
        THAW

WEDNESDAY 2ᴺᴰ MARCH 1955
 SAME TURN AND JOB BUT WITH 42383 21A.
 BERT PREECE.   NOW GOT GOOD IDEA OF ROAD.   GOOD TRIP.

THURSDAY 3 MARCH 1955
 SAME TURN AGAIN. AND 42337 (WEATHER COLD AGAIN).
 GOOD TRIP.

FRIDAY 4ᵀᴴ MARCH 1955
 SAME AGAIN AND 42383 ANOTHER GOOD TRIP.
 LOOK FORWARD TO WORKING WITH BERT PREECE AGAIN.
   GOOD MATE.   COLD.

SATURDAY 5ᵀᴴ MARCH. 1955
 STEAM RAISING ON NO 2 PIT AT SALTLEY. 3/0 ON. 11/30
        NO MATE   OFF.

A fireman's extract from his working day (J. Ford)

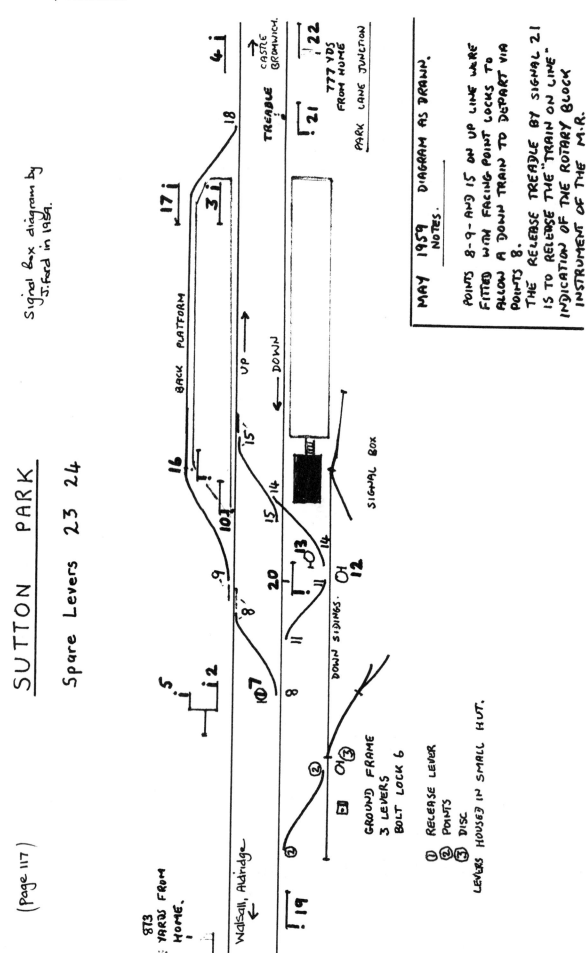

Signal box diagram by J. Ford in 1959

Inside the LCP fuels office at Sutton Park station *(John Bassett)*

The Cross City Link from the Sutton Park route *(Robert Paddison)*

Streetly in readiness for Jamboree services *(A. Spencer)*

Chapter Twelve

Penns, gone without trace

Mr. Eric Gannaway responded to my request in the Sutton Coldfield News for information about the 1879 opened station by most kindly giving me this photograph of the station in 1900. In addition to showing the uniforms of station and clothing of permanent way staff on the Midland Railway 90 or more years ago, we see Eric's uncle, Station Master E.W. North, third right on the platform, and his grandad with a cross above him. The station buildings were still very similar in the time of the last station master Mr. Les Hollins in 1965.

Station Master Ernest William North retired as Penns station master in 1934, having spent 38 years there. Eric's grandad was Edward White, the foreman platelayer at Penns. Tommy Teasdale was a member of his gang. Another Suttonian with vivid early memories of the station for Walmley is Mrs. Ethel Wassell, Mr. White's daughter, born in a cottage next to Penns station in 1905. Mrs. Wassell informed me "Penns Hall was a Wire Mill and some of the cottages for the wire workers had to be knocked down for the railway in 1879". Ethel was involved in the distribution of the newspapers that arrived by train at Penns on the 8 a.m. service.

"On a Saturday the Sutton Coldfield News and Birmingham Weekly Post were delivered. We used a truck on pram wheels and an oil lamp on the front. Out of the 50-60 houses in Walmley at the time we delivered papers to 40 houses. With the increasing number of hospital trains in the First World War to New Street, the distribution of papers by train was so disrupted we had to stop the service of local newspaper deliveries". Ethel went from Penns to Castle Bromwich on the train, changing for Leicester, Nuneaton and other locations. "We tried them all" she told me, "taking sandwiches and fruit cake with us".

So with considerable assistance from Les Hollins we take a deeper look at this station that has completely disappeared yet had some architectural features in common with Sutton Town, Sutton Park and Streetly. Streetly, Sutton Park and Penns closed on January 18th, 1965. The July, 1930 plan was prepared for rebuilding and raising platforms to standard height at Penns.

I recall that Penns in the 1950's was even quieter than Sutton Park station. One could go down the station approach from

Penns in 1900 *(Eric Gannaway)*

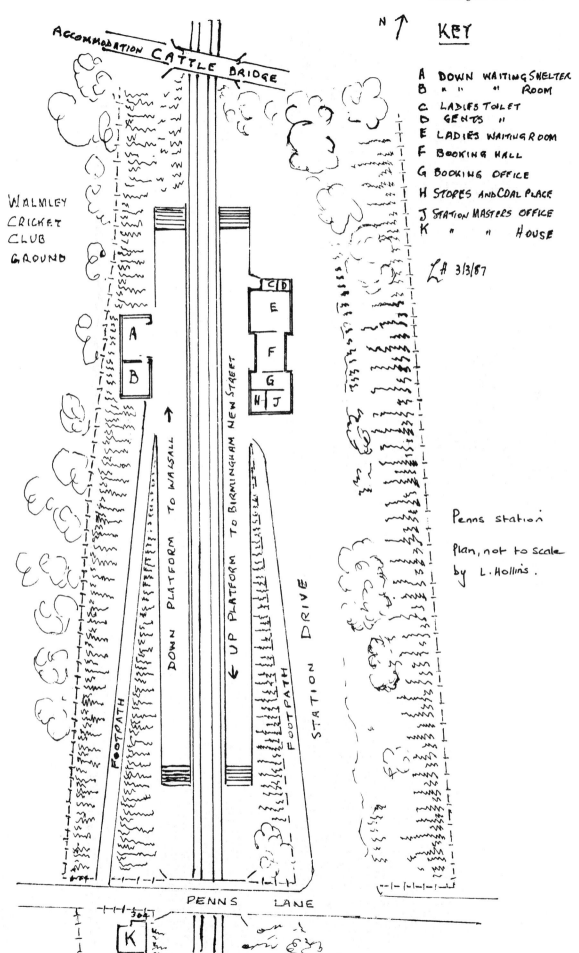

N ↑   KEY

A DOWN WAITING SHELTER
B   "   "   "   ROOM
C LADIES TOILET
D GENTS "
E LADIES WAITING ROOM
F BOOKING HALL
G BOOKING OFFICE
H STORES AND COAL PLACE
J STATION MASTERS OFFICE
K   "   "   HOUSE

LH 3/3/87

Penns station plan, not to scale by L. Hollins.

Penns station plan, not to scale (L. Hollins)

Penns station, looking towards Park Lane *(Les Hollins)*

Penns station — upside buildings towards Birmingham *(Les Hollins)*

Penns Lane to a real undisturbed country station. The only noise being the birds with trees rustling in the wind. My photograph of John Shallis on his cycle was taken on that Penns drive when he was relief station master there in August 1955.

Mr. E.S. Russell's photograph is of 42448 on 5.43 p.m Walsall–New Street service entering Penns, on June 20th 1949.

Perhaps the most well known view of the station is that seen in the Midland Bank's branch at Walmley, which was kindly loaned to me by the Manager, Mr. D.A. Spinks to include in the three week photographic exhibition in Sutton Coldfield Central Library in June, 1985.

After some seven years research more than 15 Penns photos of the passenger/goods complex of varying quality have been located.

Mr. Hollins has been extremely helpful by supplying detailed plans of Penns passenger and goods station layouts with back up photographs.

Passenger station plan

Mr. Hollins' first picture was taken from the permanent way towards Birmingham showing the upside buildings on the left and the waiting room on the downside (right) to Sutton Park and Walsall. The second view is looking at the upside buildings, with the cricket ground beyond. The road/path incline is on the righthand side.

The third shot gives more detail. The gents outside toilet is on the left. The first large window from the left is in the ladies' waiting room. The next two windows with door between is the general waiting room and booking hall. The large window on the right belongs to the booking office. The door to the booking office and the Station Master's office is visible in the second photo.

A look at the site in June, 1984, is shown under the designated Jamboree Station's section with Mr. Hollins' fourth

The 5.43 p.m. Walsall to New Street train arriving at Penns *(Eric S. Russell)*

iew, like mine taken from the Penns Lane road bridge looking owards Sutton Park.

The Station Master's house was off Penns Lane and marked "K". A shot of the Penns Lane road bridge is seen as the 6.44 New Street to Walsall service formed by a two car Gloster RCW DMU arrives on September 5th, 1959. The footpath rom the downside platform to the road bridge is visible ehind the Penns nameplate.

More detail of the upside building *(Les Hollins)*

The downside shelter is included in the photograph of the two car Park Royal DMU the same day, on the 6.54 p.m. Walsall — Birmingham New Street train. In the early days of the DMU operation first class travel was available on local services as seen in the compartment behind the driver. Former first class apartments relegated to standard class are now regularly in use on the Lichfield TV — Longbridge/Redditch cross city trains.

Staffing

In addition to the Station Master, two porters were employed with duties from 7.00 a.m. to 3.00 p.m. and the late turn from 11.30 a.m. to 7.30 p.m.

Passenger services

These were similar to those given on the focus of Sutton Park station, with six minutes allowed for the 2¼ miles between the two stations in 1952. In February, 1951, two lunchtime services on the Sutton Park line were withdrawn to save coal. The 1960 timetable journey stayed the same but the distance had increased by ¼ mile!

To Mr. Hollins the 8.25 a.m. train to Birmingham was the most important morning service. "With BR staff, 20-35

The porter receives some internal mail *(Mike Mensing)*

passengers joined that train. I wore my Station Master's hat for that train!" The 8½ miles being run in 20 minutes. It would be a well used service in getting commuters into the City for 8.45 a.m. without the frequent stopping and starting of road travel. A station at Walmley in the 1990's would be a real community asset.

Mr. Russell's picture in June, 1949, shows the commuters including 3rd class passengers returning to Penns off the 5.35 p.m. from New Street. This memory includes the larger type lamps and "Penns from Walmley" signs not around in Mr. Hollins' later sequence of shots. However, one of Mr. Hollins' predecessors apparently realised the need to have his hat on to greet the homebound passengers.

Another Penns picture taken on the day is in Douglas Jones' book on Walmley, published by Westwood Press Publications, 1990.

Penns Hall

In Mr. Hollins' career from 1958–1965 at Penns, they received few parcels from time to time but he recalls "smoked salmon coming from Penns Hall, then taken speedily to the Hall on the station bike".

Boys Brigade Annual Holiday

The annual Walmley Boys Brigade holiday necessitated the camping equipment, etc., being packed into a fitted freight wagon in the Penns goods yard and attached to the rear of a passenger train. B.B.'s Scouts, Covenanters and other Youth Groups these days normally use various forms of road vehicle to take them and heavy amounts of luggage to and from holiday but in the 1950's railways were the first choice for many.

Banking

Les related the banking system in those days for Penns was for him to put the monies in the appropriate sealed bag which was sent up to Mr. Ernest Hankin at Sutton Park on the 7.36 a.m. weekday service.

Mr. Hollins remembers booking staff on the line such as George Humpherson, now deceased, who lived in Jerome Road, Sutton Coldfield. Another clerk was now Chief Revenue Officer Bill Worship who I frequently meet around New Street station.

Station Gardens

With the co-operation of the porters, Mr. Hollins gradually saw the gardens transformed from beds of weeds to delightful, enjoyable flower beds. With persistence the station reached the standard of 2nd prize in the 1962/63 Best Kept Station competition.

Nursery person Mrs. Cook sent 15 boxes of flower seeds for her local railway station gardens when she read in a newspaper account what the B.R. staff were seeking to achieve with the annual B.R. flower allowance of 15/- (75p). There were some

Penns stationmaster (with hat on) welcomes passengers off the 5.35 p.m. from New Street (*Eric S. Russell*)

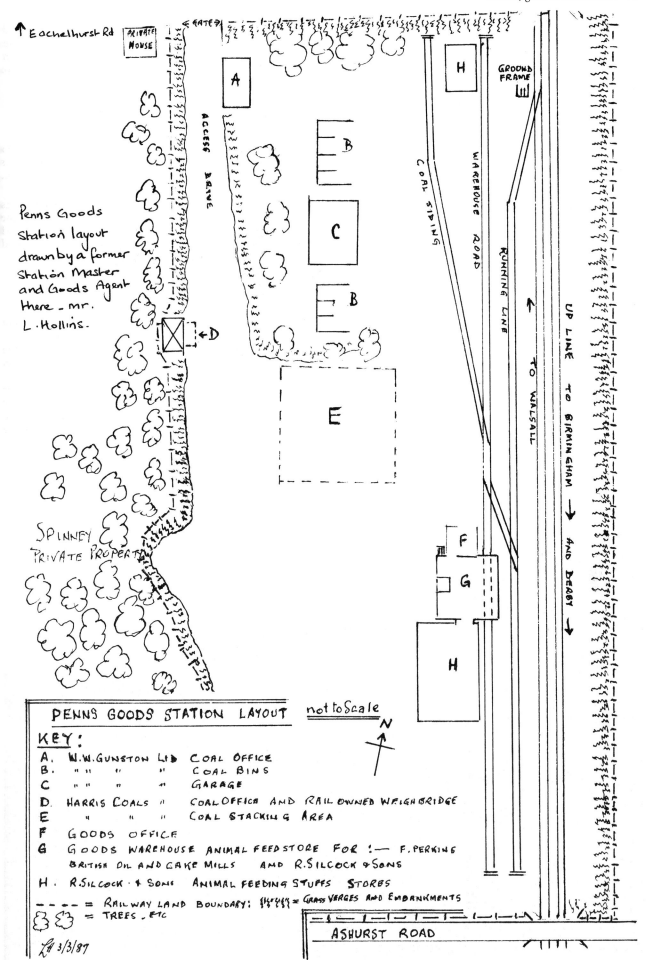

↑ Eachelhurst Rd

PRIVATE HOUSE

←GATE

A

Penns Goods
Station layout
drawn by a former
Station Master
and Goods Agent
there - mr.
L. Hollins.

ACCESS DRIVE

B

C

B

←D

E

SPINNEY
PRIVATE PROPERTY

COAL SIDING

WAREHOUSE ROAD

RUNNING LINE

TO WALSALL

UP LINE TO BIRMINGHAM AND DERBY →

H

GROUND FRAME

F

G

H

PENNS GOODS STATION LAYOUT not to Scale

N ↑

KEY:
A. W.W.GUNSTON Ltd COAL OFFICE
B.   "   "   "   "   COAL BINS
C.   "   "   "   "   GARAGE
D. HARRIS COALS "   COAL OFFICE AND RAIL OWNED WEIGHBRIDGE
E.   "   "   "   "   COAL STACKING AREA
F. GOODS OFFICE
G. GOODS WAREHOUSE ANIMAL FEED STORE FOR :— F. PERKINS
     BRITISH OIL AND CAKE MILLS   AND R. SILCOCK & SONS
H. R. SILCOCK · & SONS ANIMAL FEEDING STUFFS STORES
---- = RAILWAY LAND BOUNDARY: ⧓⧓⧓ = GRASS VERGES AND EMBANKMENTS
☘☘ = TREES . ETC

LH 3/3/87

ASHURST ROAD

Penns Goods station layout *(Les Hollins)*

surprises for the greenfingered staff when they discovered the flower seeds included carrots.

Proposed Halts

Two schemes were considered by BR and both dropped for Halts at Coles Lane and Kingsbury Road on the Castle Bromwich–Walsall line.

Although the one was to be called Coles Lane halt, the site was situated in Ebrook Road, near to our Jerome Road municipal council house. Coles Lane halt went as far as "being pegged out". Mr. Hollins submitted a supplementary inventory having forgotten a station clock and second chair. Councillor F.H. Payne, Chairman of the Borough Council's Transport Committee, "had been agitating for an improved service on the line and provision for a halt at Coles Lane" the Sutton Coldfield News reported on March 29th, 1963.

Kingsbury Road halt was proposed during the early stages of the Castle Vale development. BR hoped that the halt and Castle Bromwich Station on the Midland main line would attract patronage from at least two areas of the proposed vast municipal council housing estate.

With the hindsight of the 1990's there is certainly potential Centro customers around Castle Bromwich, Castle Vale, Penns, Coles Lane Halt, Sutton Park, and Aldridge stations. A possible earlier Midland cross city service would meet many community travel needs now.

The Penns staff in the 1950's (Les Hollins)

75022 on southbound parcels passing Penns Goods shed (Mike Mensing)

One of the regular freight services going through Penns *(Mike Mensing)*

A number of drivers at New Street have told me that there used to be a Walsall circular service between New Street — Castle Bromwich — Sutton Park — Walsall — Bescot — Soho — and back into New Street. Such a service these days would encourage more rail customers at a number of residential developments.

Proposed car-carrying services

Penns was a possible location for the proposed car-carrying services. Apparently Penns Goods Yard was seriously considered as an alternative to the eventually selected Sutton Coldfield goods site.

Mr. Hollins had a team of BR "officials from Birmingham who came down to Penns to inspect the site as the proposed new Birmingham area terminal".

Freight business

We are again indebted to Les Hollins this time for a drawing of the Penns Goods Station layout.

The interesting photograph taken of the Penns staff in the goods yard helps focus on the freight side of Penns. Standing in front of the six ton Austin, BR vehicle 544380M–WR0937 from the Aston depot are: passenger porters David Wall (who had worked at Four Oaks Station), Alfred Bianchi; Aston driver Albert Jones; Goods checker Ernie Hopwood and Station Master/Goods Agent Les Hollins. The boy kneeling on the left was a friend of Alfred and the man on the right was "Arthur".

The vehicle was designated for daily deliveries from Penns Goods. The Austin was frequently supplemented by other vehicles ex-Aston/Lawley Street. Vehicles were also hired from J. Luck and BRS as traffic increased and prior to Bank Holidays.

When the new SM arrived in 1957, about 6,500 tons of coal and patented fuels were rail moved into the goods yard, increasing considerably by the mid 1960's. W.W. Gunston was the resident coal merchant, with Harris Coal run by the Hallett family.

Animal feeding stuff was conveyed to the two Penns based dealers of Richard Silcox and Sons (liverpool) and British Oil and Coke Mills.

"Most traffic came on the weekdays T51 arriving from Water Orton approx. at 11.40 a.m. going on to Walsall Wood Colliery and returning. One saturday not long before the yard closed, 4-6-0 46110 Grenadier Guardsman was the T51 loco".

M. Mensing's shot of September 5th, 1959, gives an indication of the growing coal business as stated "4" 4-6-0 75022 passes with southbound parcels.

Thinking back to WWII and how Penns goods yard was of use then reminds me of another Driver Bill Alcock's stories. "The Penns goods yard was not very large, normally handling coal merchants traffic and animal feeds into the warehouse. But during the war it handled a lot of steel traffic for the war factories of Castle Bromwich. As the points into Penns goods yard was operated by a ground frame and not by a Signal Box, the train could not be shunted into the siding to clear the main line, to let other trains go by. With the extra traffic, and all wagons having to be reversed onto the locomotive, we were sometimes shunting for up to two hours there, with the main line blocked. Two guards on the train to assist with the shunting was tried. However it was the volume of traffic into a small goods yard that caused the delay".

This is a good clear view of the goods shed with two-car Gloster RCW DMU on the 1.46 p.m. Walsall–New Street service. The warehouse had a 13 cwt. crane.

A further Mike Mensing view at Penns is of ex-LNWR "7F" 0-8-0 49219 "plodding through Penns Station with a northbound freight", is seen on page 81.

New peaks of traffic — then closure

Mr. Hollins told me that the decision to close the Penns Goods station on February 1st, 1965 (two weeks after the withdrawal of the branch passenger services) made no sense. Apparently the revenue from the increased goods side was considerable and the goods side was closed when it had hit new peaks of traffic.

Further evidence of increased trade with the new cattle feed shed *(Mike Mensing)*

Chapter Thirteen

Sutton's Miniature and Garden Model railways

A forgotten Sutton railway is beginning to become known again through John Tidmarsh's, 1990 published "The Sutton Coldfield 15″ gauge railway" by Plateway Press. Like many other children and later young men I rode on the same Sutton Miniature Railway trains and looked through the wood fencing to see the miniature steam locos go past. Two of Mike Mensing's photographs on July 8th, 1956, gave us views of 4-4-2 No. 2 "Sutton Flyer". In the first the "Flyer" waits for us

corridor train. John Tidmarsh thought the photo dated from around 1938 when the line was relaid with track from the closed Yarmouth Miniature Railway. Mr. Nigel Parkinson, former Yarmouth owner, laid out the new track for Amusement Park owner Pat Collins. John told me "the SMR closed in 1924/5 and with the relaying and new stock re-opened in 1938". The photo also shows the signalbox and a more close up section of an amusement area. The journey took

The train returning to the terminus *(Mike Mensing)*

to leave the Crystal Palace terminus on an evening passenger (circular trip) run.

The Railway was within 10 minutes walk from Sutton Coldfield (LNWR) station and not much longer if any from Sutton Park station. A selection of Pat Collins fair attractions are on the right of the train. The second shot has the same train on the return journey passing the fencing where children within the park stood and watched the railway activity.

The third photograph looks through the terminus building at the Crystal Palace shortly after the re-opening of the 15″ gauge with a former Yarmouth Miniature Railway engine on a

about 3½ minutes on its circuit passing a number of the amusement park attractions and being a convenient way of seeing some of the park scenery around the Wyndley Pool area.

Storage

One wonders if the SMR would make a profit these days somewhere around its original site near the main town gate. John Tidmarsh advised me in 1990 that much of the SMR was still stored in Oldbury as recorded in the Sutton Coldfield News dated 27.10.1978.

DMNS operators *(John Bassett)*

A 1938 record of the SMR's re-opening *(A. Spencer)*

Rebirth

One never knows if the SMR, closed at the end of the 1962 Summer Season, will re-open, bringing steam back to Sutton Coldfield, 80 years or more after the miniature railway opened. Stranger things have happened. If Snow Hill tunnel and station can be born again, there must be hope for other financially viable railways in the Sutton Coldfield area.

DMNS

One of the most popular model railways in the Midlands will probably include the third of an acre one in Sutton Coldfield. The layout includes a scale model of New Street station and Rugeley Power Station. Two BR staff seen operating the services are senior technical officer Mark Davies and New Street station supervisor Keith Tetley, who has one of the locos named after him.

4-4-2 No. 2 "Sutton Flyer" leaving for Wyndley Pool (*Mike Mensing*)

Chapter Fourteen

Demise of Aston shed and Motorail

About nine months after my leaving BR in 1957 a car-carrying or car-sleeper service started from Sutton Coldfield to Stirling on Sunday June 1st, 1958. The 'News' reported: "The new British Railways car-sleeper train service from the Midlands to Scotland got off to a quiet but sure start from Sutton Coldfield station on Sunday evening. A Streetley man, Mr. E.H. Baxter, drove the train with a Class 5 engine (number 45038) to Derby on the first stage of its journey to Stirling on the edge of the Highlands. Aged 28, Mr. Baxter has been a railwayman since 1944. On the Sunday he was accompanied by Mr. B. Kemp, a 17 years old fireman of Nechells, Birmingham. Sutton Coldfield has been chosen as the Southern terminus rather than Birmingham because of the better railway facilities offered. Passengers sleep in compartments containing four second class sleeping berths". Packed suppers could be supplied on departure and breakfast at Stirling or Sutton Coldfields hotels on arrival. The initial services had covered accommodation for 20 cars, and 84 passengers in 2nd class sleeping berths. The

outward journeys being made from Sutton on Sundays and Wednesdays, and returning on Mondays and Thursdays, that first season from June 1st–August 31st, 1958. The return fare for car and driver was £14.10.0 with additional adults charged £5 each.

Eric Baxter the driver on the first public service car-sleeper is a Train Crew Inspector at New Street station these days and was in the Blackpool Central picture. Mr. Kemp is now a Saltley driver. Considering the importance of the service, the train crew at 28 and 17 sounded on the young side to me, but John Williams the New Street Train Crew leader found that the Aston men were frequently much younger than at other depots. In diesel loco days he with his secondman took over a train at Crewe from a much older duo. The Crewe driver was so incensed at seeing such a young whipper-snapper of a driver that he gave his handover instructions to John via his Crewe secondman. Ken Beasley throws some further light on the subject. "During the war, drivers could volunteer to stay on

70046 at Sutton Coldfield on car-carrying duties with a vehicle joining the train *(Arthur Spencer)*

until they were 70, and some did, which reduced the choice for promotion for younger men. At a number of depots like Blackpool, you could find older crews because they let promotion pass them as they ran businesses like boarding houses and put outside interests before a career".

Class "5" on the car-carrier (*John Hicks*)

This print of Arthur Spencer finds "Britannia" Class 70046 "Anzac" in 1960 on the car-carrier service at the Sutton terminal, with a car being driven into the covered van, close to the present offices of *Chess*. As a fireman, John Williams' wrists and arms swelled up from the heat of Britannia fireboxes which required the coal to be put into all the corners of the wide fire area. On the car-carrier/sleeper, the train engine John

told me "waited in the Sutton bay platform with the carriages and sleeping cars, later propelling the train near to the home signal, before drawing into the down main platform. The covered vans were backed onto the first part of the train by a Class '64' or something similar. Whilst at the down main signal, the fireman got the fire in good condition. The Aston men took the train via Lichfield City, Wychnor Junction, Burton-on-Trent to Derby where they were relieved". Bill Ramm the former Lichfield TV and later City station master advised me "when the car-sleeper in the first few years went via Wychnor Junction it required special opening of the line".

Train Crew Inspector Eric Baxter felt "he had not been chosen specially for the first trip, it was just a job in that link. The press were there, and some local rail managers but I can't remember any mayoral chains. No photographs were taken by the press. Our route was via Lichfield, Burton to Derby at the time. Some while later the Stirling went via New Street, though it was not booked to stop and on to Crewe. At Derby, Bunny Kemp and I returned passenger. The engine 45038 was an Aston loco".

The 1965 car-carrying brochure of retired signalman William Gilbert gives three services each week, both ways. The weekday train left Sutton at 8 p.m., due in 8 hours 15 minutes later, with the Sunday train taking 20 minutes less. The southbound car-sleeper departed at 10.20 p.m., arriving at 6.25 a.m. on a Sunday and 25 minutes later in the week.

John Hicks' picture has a Class "5" on the car-carrying train, showing the goods yard and goods shed in use. In 1965 the charges were:-

	Single	Return
Driver and car up to 14' 6"	£15	£22
Driver and car over 14' 6"	£16	£24
High season surcharge all cars	£1	£2
Each adult passenger	£5	£7 10s.
Each child (aged 3 under 14)	£3	£4 10s.

Height of car must not exceed 6' 6"

"The White Knight" at Aston M.P.D. waiting for its return journey on the car-carrying service (*Ted Higgs*)

The same leaflet tells potential customers that while BR "look after your car, you step into your sleeper, a comfortable bed on wheels. Carpets, lashings of hot water, a fold-down dressing table and large mirrors, clothes hangers, and — in most compartments — electric razor points. Everything you need is right here. Try the bed. Deep, well-sprung mattress. Crisp, fresh linen. Even a bedside lamp".

For those who preferred to do it a bit cheaper, the normal compartments had travel rugs and pillows supplied. "Compact Supper Boxes at 9s each" could be ordered at Sutton and Stirling.

My brother-in-law Michael once got an unexpected cab ride in the "64" type banking engine up to Four Oaks with the car-carrier service. The loco then dropped him off at Sutton Coldfield, where he went home to Tudor Hill with some explaining to do.

The 1967 Motorail brochure features many services including Sutton Coldfield to Stirling and to Newton Abbot. The West Country train left Sutton Coldfield at 11.30 p.m. arriving at 5.15 a.m., and the return service was 3.40 p.m. from Newton Abbot back in the West Midlands at 8.30 p.m., May–November.

Aston driver Ted "Buttons" Higgs gave me the print of former LNER A3 4-6-2 60077 "The White Knight" awaiting its return duty from Aston shed on the evening Motorail train to Stirling. Ted advised me that two Eastern engines had

A typical Hostel kitchen (*Muriel Higgs*)

worked the Anglo-Scottish service before it was discovered neither has sufficient clearance for the Sutton route!

Charles Warrington of the District Passenger Manager's office is frequently mentioned as one of the most involved admin persons with the service. Molly Winwood spent a number of summer seasons delegated to help on the administrative side of the West Midland car-sleeper services but worked as a Courier as well. To increase patronage on the Sutton Coldfield–Stirling train, British Railways "reserved 30–35 places on Tuesday evenings during the lighter time of the year. The compartments were made up into beds with one either side. Many preferred these sleeping arrangements to the 4-bunk sleeping compartments" said Molly. As Courier she then accompanied the group of 30 or so on a trip to the Trossachs, returning with the party to Sutton that evening on the car sleeper.

Instructor John Williams was on a 47 after the diesels had taken over from the steam locos, the service then being called Motorail with car flat wagons being used. As he sat in the cab of the diesel he saw movement on a wagon. A car was moving along the wagons driverless. John clambered onto the leading wagon running to the car to prevent it coming off. Apparently the car did not have its handbrake on and chokes had been knocked out too early by a rail person. My father-in-law, Cyril Smith advised me that he drank some spirits on the motorail train he caught, because he was apprehensive about listening to the clickety-click of the carriage all through the night. The train official told him he need not have gone to such expensive measures because once the train reached the main line, presumably at Wychnor Junction, the train would be travelling on welded track.

During the 1972 summer season more than 4,000 cars and almost 12,000 drivers and passengers were carried to Stirling, St. Austell and Newton Abbot from Sutton. However, the services finished in September 1972 "as a matter of economics".

Camden's succulent offers

John Williams told me that one Aston link involved a Birmingham — London — Liverpool — London — Birmingham parcel train sequence with stay-overs at Camden and Edge Hill. "The cook at Camden made lovely big rolly polly puddings in long tubes, with plenty of custard. As part of a three course meal the first helping of pudding was free but I was always willing to pay for seconds!" Another turn took the Aston men on freight trips from Birmingham — Liverpool — London — Liverpool — Birmingham, which resulted in them cooking their own meals as my brother recounted, at Edge Hill. Muriel Higgs' print of a Hostel kitchen typified the cooking range and saucepans found in many similar LMR premises, like Aston.

An insight into the popularity of the Blackpool illuminations to the West Midlander is illustrated by this picture taken by Ted Higgs, first left on the front row, using a time switch, of six Aston crews posing in the Blackpool central hostel canteen after a meal, prior to returning their tired passengers back home.

A number of the same train crew members are still to be seen in the Birmingham area, including radio ham (G4 CPB) Stan Walker standing behind Ted. Eric Baxter is fourth on the left of the front row men. The Aston and Monument Lane men, similar to thousands of footplate staff throughout the country saw the change over from steam to diesel power and for some to electric in the 1960s. Stan Walker recalls "that all steam had left Aston by early 1965".

Ken Beasley, an LDC man at the time noted that when the "new Birmingham New Street booking-on point was established, it included 77 men from Aston, 73 from Monument Lane and men from a number of other depots all over the country. It took two years to get everyone trained up

to the necessary standard, and familiarity with the varied types of traction". Stan Walker finished at Aston MPD as a Running Shift Foreman at 1400 hours on Sunday March 5th, 1967 starting as a Train Crew Inspector at New Street at 0600 hours, the next morning on March 6th. "When we reported for duty, many people did not know where we were to be housed on New Street station", said Stan.

John Williams' print recaptures the explosion that toppled the mighty Aston shed coaling plant, "which was one of the first of that type", Mrs Higgs informed me. It's at times of dramatic change that a neutral person like a Railway Chaplain can be of assistance to railway people. More recently I had the privilege to spend time with Stourbridge Junction men before, during and after the closure of their depot. Something of the men's feelings, sadness and hopes was communicated through a BBC TV Midlands Today mini documentary.

3D Ghost

One person I never met but I understand still haunts the Aston 3D site, at Bristol Motors is an old bearded loco driver with a hat and an oil lamp he swings around about 7-7.30 a.m. some misty mornings.

Aston crews take a break at Blackpool central hostel (*Ted Higgs*)

Demolition of Aston MPD coaling plant (*John Williams*)

Chapter Fifteen

Lichfield and Park Line passenger closures

My four years working with boys and their families as a Junior Covenanter leader in Sutton Coldfield gradually made me aware of the need that some young people and parents did benefit from support and encouragement in bringing up their families, by youth leaders. With the Juco group continuing to flourish I moved into full-time social work in 1961, taking a position in Lichfield, working with boys on remand from Juvenile Courts. The year and half there helped me recognise the limited amount of knowledge and training I had in supporting very difficult individuals at times. During a weekend two staff worked through from 7 a.m. on the Saturday morning to 1 p.m. on a Monday lunchtime. The weekend programme my former Army officer colleague and I pursued included a lot of outside activities, games and long walks. On the Sunday afternoon during a fairly long walk we told the 28 lads to sit down and have a rest. The other supervisor said to me quietly, "John, we could certainly do with a few less than this number to keep an eye on". I agreed. A few minutes later one of the juniors shouted to us "Sirs, some seniors have gone away". "Well tell them to come back",

barked my colleague. "They can't hear me now" said the delighted youngster, full of admiration for his elder courageous remandees. With a knowledge that the lads were always trying to get each other into trouble, we looked over the wall and sure enough some distance away could be seen five youths having trouble getting across a ploughed field. While my mate rounded up the remaining 23, I ran to the nearest telephone box, informing the superintendent of the incident.

Most of the supervisors and the teaching staff included subjects in the evenings that a group of boys would enjoy. I wrote to Sir Alfred Owen, who kindly brought along a film about his BRM racing cars and talked with the lads about his involvement in the venture. Some of the activities were combined with the girls, housed the other side of the playground. Apparently my writing to Sir Alfred as a friend caused the Home's superintendent some official rebuff, because unknown to me, Sir Alfred was the chairman of Staffordshire County Council, my employer, and should have been invited by the appropriate sub-committee chairperson! I

46135 under burnt out Lichfield TV HL *(Peter Myatt)*

offered my apologies to the boss who said with a smile, "as you invited Sir Alfred who has agreed to come, it would be discourteous for me to stop him!" On reflection the chairman probably got a better insight of the work of the home than if he went on an official visit. It probably did not do my boss's later requests for additional resources any harm either!

For the good of the boys of course, many found themselves taken on walks that somehow went via the Trent Valley railway route. A group of spotters can be seen on the TV cattle dock as Patriot 45538 "Giggleswick" crosses over onto the down main, page 92.

Looking at this picture Trent Valley signalman Les Starkey, a former Lichfield Cathedral chorister, advised me that "the first line off on the left went into the maltings and waterworks. The railway put the vans of grain in for them and wagons of coal for the waterworks. A horse was employed on the private sidings. With the horse and turntable the vans and wagons could be put where required". Les noticed that trains on the connecting line, from the low to the high level, "frequently needed sand on the rails to get a grip. Sometimes", he continued, "the train came back when unsuccessful for a second try". It was 375 yards between TV Junction and TV Low Level No. 1 signal boxes with a 20 mph restriction, according to the Sectional Appendix 1960.

A further incident that a number of railway staff and the local community can bring to mind is the fire on the high level station. Workmen are at the scene in the print by local photographer Bill Kinnear.

When talking to the duty signalperson at Lichfield Trent Valley Low Level signal box it can be very alarming for the first few visits to feel the building sway as a train passes at speed either on the up or down fast lines. Relief Signalman Geff Brookes was told when he started on the TV line in 1967 "by the district Signalling Inspector (DSI) that the box was due to come out shortly". A number of staff have informed me that the LL box has been condemned for many years. Geff continued "0300 hours one morning in 1984 as a freightliner passed at speed on the down main there was a flashing of the overheads and a definite crack with movement on the window frames". He later found wood over the whole length of the box. Eventually the train stopped at Norton Bridge so the driver may have felt the pulling of the load. Regrettably, I quite expect to hear that a train has hit the box as it passes at 110 mph. The most serious Lichfield mishap as the railways call an accident happened at Lichfield TV station on New Year's Day 1946. Adrian Vaughan in "Obstruction Danger" covers the accident on pages 89-99, using some of Eric Russell's pictures of the locality, with plans and drawing. The book is published by Patrick Stephens Ltd., Glasgow, 1989. Adrian as a former BR signalman includes technical know-how in his cautionary tales of over 30 British railway accidents.

Other things that occurred when I worked in Lichfield was Bill Kinnear's move. He explains, "I moved from Scotland to work in the Shenstone signal box. It still had a fairly busy goods yard and many commuters to both Birmingham and Lichfield were able to make use of the half hourly service of diesel multiple units which provided the passenger service. A sketch of the track layout from memory shows the basic details but I cannot claim 100 per cent accuracy as far as the goods yard trackwork is concerned, but it will give a general outline to the reader. Scheduled freight traffic was sparse with a solitary out and back working from Aston to Wychnor with coal for Aston Gasworks and this was usually worked by 8F 2-8-0s with the crews changing at Wychnor. Occasionally a 9F 2-10-0 would appear and on a couple of days the loaded train passed, hauled by an LNW G2 0-8-0. The trip freights on the line provided a fair amount of interest since Shenstone was the exchange point for the Sutton line trip and pick-up working from Burton and this took place around lunchtime. Hauled by a 4F or Stanier 2-6-0 the Sutton line trip was first on the scene and shunted the yard as required before making a dash up to Blake Street to serve the small yard at that station. Normally

Shenstone station with signal box in distance *(Bill Kinnear)*

the Burton goods would arrive while the Blake Street job was being done collecting any traffic for the north and leaving any wagons for the Sutton line. Burton shed provided the loco for this working and again 4F 0-6-0s appeared regularly as did "Crab" 2-6-0s including the locos fitted with rotary poppet valves.

"One other use to which this yard at Shenstone was put concerned the rebuilding of many bridges during the electrification of the Birmingham area and much prefabrication of bridge decks was done in the yard and this brought engineers trains and also the breakdown cranes from Derby and Bescot to provide the lifting power necessary to handle the massive concrete beams. The other notable service on the line was the Sutton Coldfield to Stirling car sleeper train. This was timed to pass southbound before the signalbox opened, although late running sometimes gave the chance to see it rush the three mile climb to Butlers Lane with a Royal Scot or Jubilee on the front".

On March 3rd, 1962, Mrs. Helen Ramm took one of her annual parties by rail up to Euston but this time at her request BR came up with the highly polished "City of Lichfield" 46250, the 8P Princess Coronation Class Locomotive, seen off from Trent Valley by the Major, Councillor W. Richards. The engine was christened at the same station in 1942. At Euston, as seen in the William Ramm's picture, Mrs. Ramm is making

46250 "City of Lichfield" at Euston *(William Ramm)*

"Giggleswick" at Lichfield TV (*F.R. Morten*)

a presentation to the footplate crew, with some of the 420 passengers enjoying the occasion. William, Mr. and Mrs. Bill Ramm's son, was the youngest person to be given the job of a BR Initial Electrical Inspector at Crewe. Tragically he died at work.

The Lichfield Bowers continued to be popular. Arthur Attenborough informed me "that the four upside roads were completely emptied of all coal wagons so they could be available for passenger traffic. 20,000-30,000 came in by train, and it took two days to sort out the used tickets and send off to Derby". Another annual entertainment was the Big Top coming to the city by train. In William Ramm's print one of Chipperfield's Circus elephants is checking the Lichfield City cattle dock before venturing out to join a parade. Based on my own cleaning out experiences at Four Oaks, after such animals the local staff had some hard work in front of them.

In Mr. Ramm's further print some machinery is seen on a tripper that has probably been brought at Winterton's monthly second hand sale of farm equipment and going to Welsh farmers, who apparently purchased a lot of items from the Lichfield sales.

Another feature to change in years to come was the rebuilding of Blake Street as an important boundary station of the WMPTE area. John Hicks shares three shots of the former LNWR station, somewhat different from Eric Russell's 1956 picture.

The experiences at the Lichfield Home made me aware that preventative help should be the type of service that I would prefer to offer. It was also while I worked at Lichfield that another work called the Fellowship Hour at Duke Street Chapel, Sutton Coldfield appeared to be meeting a need for senior citizens, in an effort to prevent them from feeling unwanted and undervalued.

Although my next social work post was only temporary while someone was away on a professional training course, it gave more experience. Joan and I who married in that year had to trust God with our future, as only four months later my job ceased. Our Christian friends at Duke Street continued to support us with Mr. Jack Frith allowing us to rent one of his terraced houses almost next door to Duke Street Chapel. In God's timing a permanent post came up in January 1964, in Derbyshire. As a social worker, I specialised in work with

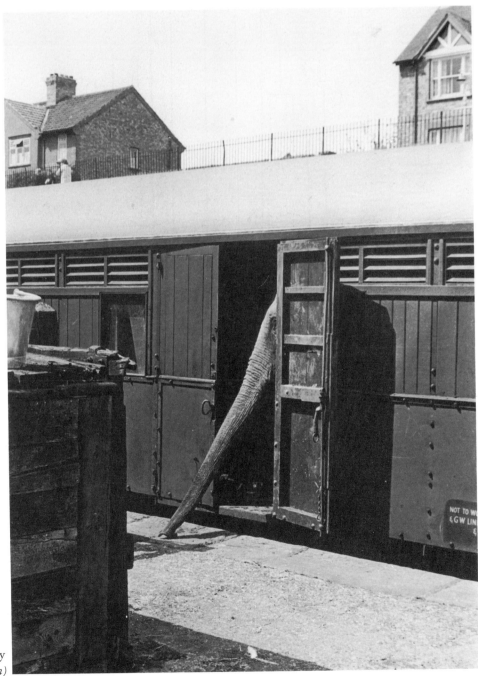

Elephant truck, Lichfield City
(William Ramm)

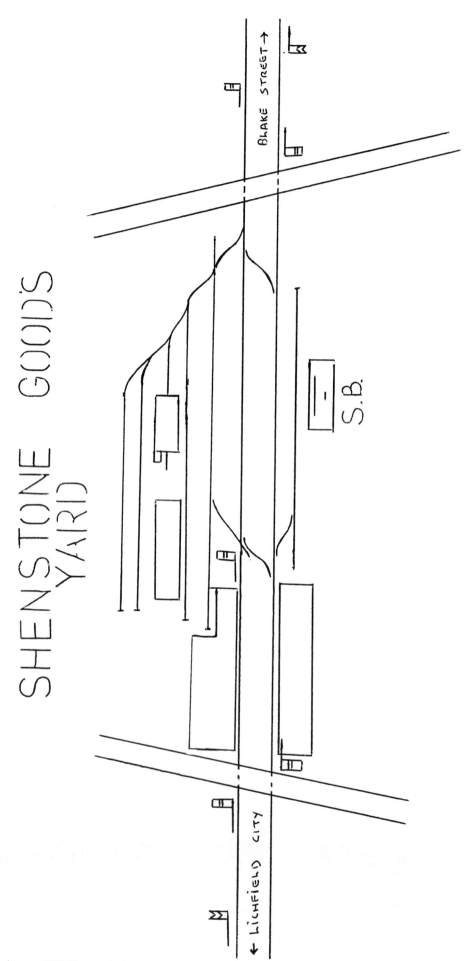

SHENSTONE GOODS YARD

BLAKE STREET →

S.B.

← LICHFIELD CITY

Track layout *(Bill Kinnear/John Williams)*

J.N. WILLIAMS
BIRMINGHAM ROAD LEARNING SCHOOL.

families, youths, fostering and adoption. The local authority seconded me to university to complete a full-time professional course for experienced staff. Between 1964 and 1985 we lived in Derbyshire and south London, returning to the West Midlands in January, 1985. Thanks to many co-contributors within the general community and railway industry some significant events have been included in Cross City Connections. One such occasion was the replacing of the railway bridge at Chester Road in April, 1964. The photograph provides a close-up of the Crewe-based steam crane.

Staying at Chester Road a little longer, one recalls the unexpected bonus for steam enthusiasts in the early 1960s when locomotive hauled non-corridor stock trains returned on rush hour services due to difficulties with DMU units. Arthur Spencer's print shows 45058 pulling into Chester Road with a New Street bound train. I am not sure what happened when steam made that short reappearance on the passenger trains, but in the 1980/90s when DMUs/sprinters are not available and diesel locomotives take over, the trains are frequently full with enthusiasts. From my New Street station office windows I have seen such goings-on with Hereford services powered by 31s, Cardiff with 37s and when visiting Derby seen that local service to Crewe with a pair of 20s in charge. One of the most interesting services I have heard announced at New Street was in 1989 when the half hourly service during the day to Euston was disrupted by some problem with the overhead electric equipment. An intriguing alternative service was announced to London, not to Paddington as I expected but to St. Pancras. The traction I noted was a Class 58.

Many folk tell me how they regret not taking pictures of the steam days, but fortunately many did including the recording of locomotives at the end of their days such as Richard Thorne's print of 42790, 42417 and 42419 standing in the snow at Saltley. A pasttime for some people is to recall prices "in the old days" so here is a selection of special Day Tickets in September, 1964. Some were not available until after 9.30 a.m.

Sutton line tripper with second hand farm equipment *(William Ramm)*

on weekdays: *Aldridge* to New Street 4/1, Bloxwich 2/5, Willenhall 2/7. *Blake Street* to: Adderley Park 4/10, Lichfield City 2/2; *Butlers Lane* to: Aston 3/1, Stechford 5/3; *Castle Bromwich* to: Hinckley 7/6, Leicester (London Road) 12/11, Repton and Willington 10/8; *Four Oaks* to: Berkswell 8/3, Lichfield TV 3/8; *Kingsbury* to: Barnt Green 8/2, Coleshill 1/11, Tamworth 2/7; *Lichfield City* to Alrewas 2/4, Brownhills 2/5, Hammerwich 1/7, Hednesford 7/6, Walsall 3/11; *Lichfield TV* to Burton-on-Trent 4/9, Nuneaton (TV) 7/9, Rugeley Town 3/7; *Penns* to: Cannock 6/5, Wolverhampton (HL) 5/10; *Sutton Coldfield* to: Coventry 9/9, New Street 3/-; *Sutton Park* to: Darlaston 3/11, and Wyrley and Cheslyn Hay 5/7.

Crewe North steam crane at Chester Road *(Richard Thorne)*

Blake Street before
rebuilding
(John Hicks)

Three engines at Saltley *(Richard Thorne)*

45058 on DMU substitute at Chester Road *(Arthur Spence)*

Pines departure (*J. Haddock*)

6755 at Aldridge (*W.A. Camwell*)

Speculation about the future of the Sutton Park line had been going on for years, but one proposal seems to have got lost in the haze of distant years. The Railway Executive in February 1958 proposed a two hour interval service between Birmingham (New Street) and Walsall via Sutton Park probably by the popular recently introduced DMUs. This was a probable RE response to the strong negotiations going on with the Sutton Coldfield Borough Council for an improved train service supported by a petition by local businessmen and a leaflet pepared by Aldridge Urban District Council. A look at Aldridge station in 1935 Midland days is provided by Mr. W.A. Camwell, showing former LNW 2-4-2T 6755 in LMS red livery, on a Birmingham-Walsall train. Alongside the demand for more trains on the Park line the Railways were being asked to provide halts at East View Road and Kingsbury Road. Mr. Hollins' memories of the proposed halt between Sutton Park and Penns was the under bridge that leads to playing fields off Ebrook Road. People fighting for a halt at Kingsbury Road bridge (A38) said "if one is built it will be the first time Minworth will have an adequate transport service to Sutton Coldfield". Presumably they meant if the two hour interval timetable operated from Kingsbury Road.

In between the February information and the next details in November 1958 "the Government had placed a restriction on railway expenditure which forestalled the anticipated additional services and likely opening of the East View Road"/ Ebrook Road Halt. The report suggested that the RE may still "grant an East View Road Halt under a line review". Figures in the 1960s for the passenger traffic on the Park line was: "mean average traffic of 43,750 passengers per annum", using the four trains each day, five each way on Saturdays. Figures for individual stations revealed that more than half of the line's travellers used Streetly.

Station	Annual average	Each weekday	Saturdays
Streety	23,480	80-90	50
Sutton Park	8,610	30-40	20
Penns	11,480	40-60	20-30

With the inevitable loss of the Park passenger services would go the summer sights of the Pines Express, seen preparing to leave Walsall with a 4-6-0 Jubilee 45662 "Kempenfelt" in charge. The second portion engine, another Jubilee, is in the background. The photographer Mr. J. Haddock has had photographic exhibitions of his railway prints in the West Midlands. A reminder of tripper 64 on the Sutton Park route is caught here by a BR print given to me by the late John Ford, at Aldridge with the box and station in the background.

There was a lobby of opinion in and around Sutton who wanted the Park line to completely close if it lost the passenger traffic. The News Editor commented "surely it cannot be said that the line detrimentally affects the amenities of the park?" The line closed to regular passenger services on January 18th, 1965, the same day as passenger services were withdrawn on the Wolverhampton (High Level)–Walsall–Lichfield City/TV–Burton route. Had the Sutton Park line closed to all traffic a Railway Preservation Society expressed interest to "choose the 4½ miles section from Aldridge to Sutton Park as the most convenient for our purposes" to make it a pleasure steam line "for weekends and holiday periods given the necessary financial support.".

Tripper 64 powered by D 5233 at Aldridge (British Railways)

Chapter Sixteen

Cross City Link

Apparently things were not all well with the income from the Four Oaks line at off-peak times because British Rail proposed to make eight stations unstaffed at such times from January 2nd, 1967. The stations were: Shenstone, Blake Street, Butlers Lane, Four Oaks, Wylde Green, Chester Road, Erdington and Gravelly Hill. The railway management were probably facing mounting costs of the Rugby–Birmingham–Stafford electrification scheme, and trying to curb expenditure in other areas of West Midland operation. In John Williams' colour print, progress can be seen at the New Street station site, with a manual signal box still intact, and the overhead wires still to come. An enthusiastic Irish Catholic man working on the New Street site put up a number of crosses within the brickwork and some still remain.

Although there was some disruption with the passenger services on the WCML during the electrification, the railways continued to cooperate with Helen Ramm in the running of her annual excursions to London. The late Mr. William Ramm's picture of Lichfield residents waiting to start their rail journey from Trent Valley includes views of the progress made up to then on the change over to electric services. Mr. Bill Ramm informed me that the trains run in years when the electrification was going ahead meant passengers arrived or started from alternative London Termini to Euston.

Lichfield railway staff

Looking back to his years in charge as station master at Lichfield Trent Valley and later in the City, Bill Ramm recalls the following staff included:

Lichfield Trent Valley: Booking clerks Jeff Webb, Del Pritchard; *Signalling staff* No. 1 Box (present one) Jack Pritchard (Del's father), Ted Brazier, Bill Wallace; *Train recorders* who were Junior Porters George Ridsdale, Roy Biggin (now in rail management), Brian Matthews, No. 2 Box Signalman Petitt and Jack Shone.

Hademore Bill Pugh, Les Starkey (now at Lichfield TV) and Cyril Lewis.

Yard There were two Head Shunters — Albert Smith who lived in a TV railway cottage and Ted Dolman, who resided in Alrewas.

Lichfield City Bill moved after six years service at TV to Lichfield City in 1956 taking over from Mr. E. Norris who retired. Mr. Ramm remained as SM at the City until 1970, when he was made Area Manager. The staff Bill remembers include: *Foreman* Ted Usherwood, Ted Price; *Shunters* Jack Price, known for tennis interests; *Passenger Guards* Jack Hair, Bob Sillitoe, Frank Knight and Harry Silvester. Bob and Harry are railway staff I recall from my days on the Four Oaks line. Mr. Ramm describes the Lichfield City guards as "autocratic sort of people, proud LNWR men". *Booking Office*: the Chief Clerk was Norman Fowles, with Keith Twynham. Derek Collins worked to Mr. Ramm in management. While Mr. Ramm was in charge at the City, Bill Kinnear took the photograph of a peak on a northbound steel empties and a D200 on a local trip working. The photograph shows a crane at work in the yard, and the north end signal box now gone.

Moving with Mr. Ramm into the 1970s, we have already traced the closure of the Motorail and now have a shot of the Sutton box and the M7 gang hut in the mid-1970s looking towards Wylde Green. Towards the end of 1975 Sir Alfred Owen died at Sutton Coldfield Cottage Hospital. A stroke in 1969 had enforced him into partial withdrawal from some public service. Sir Alfred died at the age of 67.

From 1972 Joan, our son Anthone and I lived in South London, attending a chapel in Carshalton, Surrey. Again as a Junior Covenanter leader I attended some camps and houseparties for the boys. The national committee for the JUCOs agreed to my proposal to run an annual railway holiday for JUCOs 10-13 years, which we did from 1979–1983, using Derby, Crewe, Bristol and Wimbledon as our bases. It was through the indoor camping I came into contact with the Railway Mission an evangelical Christian group

New Street progress *(John Williams)*

which had been formed in 1881 to work with rail staff and their families. Two of the holidays were based at Churches supporting the Mission at Davenport Road Evangelical Church, Derby and Gresty Road Evangelical Church, Crewe.

Cross City Link

In 1973 an idea was being considered to join the south and north of Birmingham by a cross city link, not unlike the one I proposed using the Midland routes but this one from Lichfield via Sutton Coldfield to New Street and on via Longbridge to Redditch. With the re-drawing of the "boundaries the idea of a new Redditch–Birmingham–Lichfield line was ditched". In its place a Cross City Link from Four Oaks–Longbridge via New Street, all within the West Midland Passenger Transport Executive area, with WMPTE funding was pursued. The change over to the CCL "cost nearly £8m with another £1.6m being spent expanding the Tyseley rail depot". Seventy-six 3-coach diesel trains operated that service and other local services. When the service began in May 1978 "new stations had already been built at Longbridge, University and Five Ways, with rebuilding complete at Selly Oak, Bournville, Kings Norton and Northfield. Car parking was increased from 60–200 at Four Oaks and 17–100 at Sutton Coldfield".

Lichfield TV. Passengers waiting for Mrs. Ramm's special *(William Ramm)*

Peak going through Lichfield City *(Bill Kinnear)*

Erdington signal box *(Rob Selvey)*

Signals were respaced between Aston and Four Oaks, and new colour light signals introduced, taking 18 months and funded through the £8m. The through journey time was 53 minutes. On May 12th, the personal view by Penman in the Sutton Coldfield News commented about the new service under the title "Full steam ahead City". The article concludes "who knows, we might even see the return of those beautiful, yet abandoned, steam engines. Who knows, we might again one day see them, shuffling through Sutton Park, with a passenger train in tow". One of the additional benefits from the WMPTE survey into travelling patterns in Sutton and Streetly was the remodelling of the bus services with interchanges taking place at rail stations. One such service was a direct bus service from Walmley to Chester Road station.

The public quickly responded positively to the cross city link services but it was not long before the intense running of

Men crossing lines near Sutton Box *(Richard Thorne)*

the reasonably old DMUs took its toll by late running and cancellations. Even so the service became more successful, attracting many first time rail travellers by a selection of WMPTE/BR tickets. With the focus on the need for improved signalling equipment the manual box at Erdington seen in August, 1980 would not see the decade out. Visiting the rather cramped power box at Erdington, Signalman Victor Churton made me aware of his relative Edward Churton the owner of a publishing company in London in the 19th century. In 1851 he published his own work "The Rail Road Book of England". Under the *Birmingham to Leeds* heading he mentions "Sutton Coldfield is 4½ miles from Castle Bromwich. The Royal Borough is a model town and parish, in the county of Warwick, of considerable antiquity having been of some note in the Saxon times". On the other hand Lichfield TV is given "as one of the principal stations on the Stafford and Rugby branches of the LNWR, situated on a plain and generally well built".

Signalman Churton has accumulated quite a library of works by his distinguished ancestors.

Chapter Seventeen

Supporting rail staff and families

Visiting different railway locations with the boys and leaders on the JUCO railway holidays I began to mix with rail people and families again, the first time for 25 years or more. With the agreement of the General Committee of the Railway Mission, and the encouragement of an Area Manager on the Southern Region I visited six stations each month with the Mission's free 4-page monthly newspaper, the "Railway Signal". Some staff told me "to get lost" they did not want any contact with an Associate Railway Chaplain, they "were quite sure where their future lay and it certainly had nothing to do with God". A few of those did find time eventually to share their concerns with me as a neutral person.

Full time Chaplaincy

Coming up to 10 years as a Regional Training Officer with the Children's Society I had managed to complete two successful courses, one in adult education teaching and the other as a trainer. Finding the railway visiting satisfying, I prayed for an opportunity to become a full-time Railway Chaplain in the West Midlands. In addition to the useful experience gained in South London three further things happened which helped to confirm the call. Unknown to me at the time the LMR HQ with more than 1,000 staff would shortly be moving to Birmingham, requests were being received by the Railway Mission for a chaplain presence in the Midlands. Thirdly, a motto card from the Derbyshire Village Mission for the next year was sent to Joan and me. The two verses on the card said: "The Lord is there . . . come now let us leave". We accepted the challenge and promise to return to the Midlands, though we understand for some their guidance comes in different ways. A further need for our son to find accommodation near his work in Surrey was overcome. The selling of the house was going fine, then everything stopped. We were perplexed but God showed His care when Joan needed urgent surgery. The housing delay enabled her to have the treatment and some rest

Deceased driver Eric Goode's memorial (*Daphne Williams*)

before we moved in January, 1985, after three months full time in the Southern Region as a Railway Chaplain.

Since 1985 I have been relearning the railway geography in the Midlands. Even places visited since 1985 have closed and staff at all levels moved or made redundant. The greatest problem for so many rail people is that the apparent constant change. As soon as one change has been completed another starts. I share with our staff, changes are happening in all

Thank-you Buffet (*John Bassett*)

progressive industries, but it still takes grit for them to come through. With an office provided by BR at New Street I feel privileged to meet railway people in the Midlands at their work place.

Colwich memorial

When I was called out at the Colwich accident in September, 1986 I again felt privileged to see representatives of the many departments working together to get the train services reinstated. It was a humbling experience to be invited and lead a short dedication service at the Colwich Junction line side to driver Eric Goode of Crewe who died in the two-train mishap. Jan Glasscock the Area Manager at crewe arranged for the dedication stone, and Alf Taylor, the Permanent Way Supervisor in the area, organised for the two duplicate name plates of "The City of Milton Keynes" to be obtained and sited either side of the memorial in the garden he had designed and made.

With Joan's support we were able to thank railway people for the provision of the New Street office and the picture shows staff from the station and LMR HQ sharing in a "thank you" buffet. Looking at the group reminds me of the shortness of life, noting people who have since died. Again with Joan's catering skills we have run seminars, one on alcoholism in the GM's conference suite at Birmingham in an effort to support managers faced with a growing problem in all industries including the railway.

Going round the depots, signal boxes, travelling on the trains brings back memories of the steam days. In 1989 waiting on Lichfield High Level for a New Street service was one such

LRPG charter train for Barmouth arriving at the recently opened Lichfield TV High Level station *(LRPG)*

members are working at securing new passenger services to Alrewas, Barton and Burton-on-Trent, and also to Walsall. Three achievements they feel able to say are to due to LRPG are:

(1) ghost trains that were extended to Lichfield for customers turning an hourly service into every 15 minutes.

(2) the extension of the Cross City Link trains to Lichfield Trent Valley on November 28th, 1988, and

(3) the reintroduction of the Sunday service to Lichfield City which enables people to get to church if they wish.

The group has run a number of successful charter trains each year for customers along the TV and Sutton lines. The trains also pick up as far away as Derby and Cheltenham.

Cross City Link Electrification

The group's top priority was achieved in February, 1990 with Mr. Parkinson's announcement in Parliament of the electrification of the Cross City line. David MacIntosh, the Provincial Manager East and West Midlands, advised me that the full electric services could commence in 1992. The funding is coming from the West Midlands PTE and British Rail. The only small section at present electrified is between New Street and Aston. It is anticipated the new service will cut up to seven minutes from the Redditch–Birmingham timings and nine minutes off the New Street–Lichfield section. Two of the Lichfield City staff display a poster that had been at the station some weeks prior to Mr. Parkinson's statement. The electrification had been predicted with certainty as early as 1962, to be completed in that decade. The prediction was made by the mayor, Councillor Frank Brassington. John Tidmarsh told me he walked and measured the Sutton Coldfield–Lichfield line upto and including Wychnor Junction sidings in the early 1960s ready for an electrified service. So the 1990s electrification will be the second serious attempt to bring a modern electric service to Sutton and Lichfield in 30 years.

Lampman duties

With the electrification scheme, railway commuters in the Lichfield area will witness the final phase of manual signals

occasion. A man let out his pigeons for a practice flight. Years ago on the railways, thousands of pigeon baskets went by rail. Four Oaks being on the edge of the countryside frequently had the job of letting out the pigeons and noting down the time they were released. Some porters regrettably did not seem to think and let the birds out with the basket facing wires or other nearby objects that forced the pigeons to take hasty avoiding action, and sometimes getting separated from the other birds. The man I spoke to about his pigeons knew of the previous railway service but lorries now take the birds for races and practice flights. However, he seemed to appreciate that the Lichfield TV high level site gave the pigeons an elevated start.

Lichfield Rail Promotion Group

One community group which has done a lot since it was formed on February 3rd, 1985 is the Lichfield Rail Promotion Group. David Woodcock the LRPG Secretary told me the

Announcement of the Cross City electrification scheme *(John Bassett)*

being replaced by modern signalling equipment. The railway photographer and enthusiast may regret the end of the old signals but the drivers have for many years preferred the clear distinct information they pick up from the modern aspect signals, usually seen further away than with the oil lamp version. In 1990, a lampman as mentioned in stories about Sutton Coldfield, LNWR, can be witnessed taking out the freshly filled oil lamps to a number of signals in the Lichfield City and TV vicinity, but not for much longer. The electrification of the line will bring with it further electric signals and demise of the signal boxes on the Sutton Coldfield route, to be taken over by a new power box. Back in 1962 the Tamworth based Lampman's duties for the week were:

Monday Elford and Coton crossing 8.0-4/0.

Tuesday Tamworth High Level and Water Trough 8.0-4/0.

Wednesday Tamworth Low Level and Kettlebrook Sidings 8.0-4/0.

Thursday Lichfield High and Low Levels and Burton Road crossing 7.10-5/25.

Friday Rugeley and Brereton sidings 7.10-5/25.

Saturday Home station 8.0-12 noon.

That roster, dated 1.11.62 was shown to me by Ken Biggs still frequently seen on relief duties at Tamworth and Lichfield TV. Two further gems of information from about the same time that Ken passed on to me concern trains that local people used at Tamworth:

6.10 Tamworth–Coventry During the winter months the 6.10 must be provided with a *full and clean* tail lamp M-F.

1M44 6/50 Glasgow–Euston When the above train is waiting connections, it must be drawn clear of the up fast main line, to allow other traffic to pass, and *set back to siding* if necessary.

Much modernisation has taken place at Four Oaks station prior to electrification *(Rob Selvey)*

Calendar presentation *(Ron Duggins/Matlock Mercury)*

Railway Mission Calendars

One of the most busy but enjoyable times of the year is the taking and sending out the Railway Mission calendars which are free to active and retired railway staff, but non-rail people kindly send in a donation and SAE.

The print from the Matlock Mercury shows me presenting a complimentary copy of the calendar to Mrs. Sarah Rogers, a widow whose husband was a clerk of works at New Street station for the electrification programme. Her son Mick looks on.

1990's changes

The new decade of the 1990s has brought some wanted and unwanted changes. In the September 1990 issue of the Railway Magazine, page 613, there were artist's impressions of the Hunslet TIL class 323 electric multiple unit in midline livery, and an idea of what the interior will be of the cross city line trains. Of the 37 units ordered, 18 are expected to be allocated to the Redditch-Lichfield services. A most unwelcome change

for Lichfield was the I.R.A. murder committed at the city station. As a railway chaplain with counselling responsibilities to rail staff, one realises that even if the media forget the event after a couple of days, staff around may need support for a long time afterwards.

40 years on

When I joined the railways in the 1950s I had no thought of writing down my experiences. But 40 or more years later it is an encouragement to know that God can use those valley and mountain top experiences to assist other people. Cross City Connections has recorded many changes on a number of railway routes. Rob Selvey's 1990 print reminds me of the recent structural changes to the Four Oaks upside building. Those changes are an indicator of further changes to be expected on our local railway lines and in our own lives in the last decade of the twentieth century. As a Christian it is a comfort to have Hebrews 13 : 8 to hold onto in the face of more disturbing changes: "Jesus Christ is the same yesterday and today and forever".